Keep smiling!
Love
Mary Marcelento

Also by Mary Marcdante

Books
My Mother, My Friend

Postcards Books
Inspiring Words for Inspiring People

Audio
My Mother, My Friend
Living with Enthusiasm

Contributing Author
A Woman's Way to Incredible Success in Business
Chicken Soup Christmas Treasury
Chicken Soup for the Mother's Soul
Chicken Soup for the Mother's Soul 2
Chicken Soup for the Pet Lover's Soul

Living with Enthusiasm

How the 21-Day Smile Diet Can Change Your Life

Mary Marcdante

Inspired Life Publishing Company
Del Mar, California

Living with Enthusiasm: How the 21-Day Smile Diet Can Change Your Life

For information, contact:

Inspired Life Publishing Company
P.O. Box 2529
Del Mar, CA 92014

For information regarding special discounts for bulk purchases or to purchase signed gift copies, contact Mary Marcdante at 888-600-3421 or info@marymarcdante.com

ISBN 0-9727712-0-4

10 9 8 7 6 5 4 3 2 1

Bliss Quota by Peter Rengel reprinted with permission

Copy Editing by Barbara McNichol Editorial <www.barbaramcnichol.com>

Creative Editing by C. Leslie Charles <www. lesliecharles.com>

Proofreading by Laurie Gibson <wordworker1@earthlink.net >

Page design and cover and page layout and composition by Robert Goodman, Silvercat®, San Diego, California <info@silvercat.com>

Printed in the United States of America

Dedication

To my father Bob,
whose presence taught me to go for the gusto.

To my mother Grace,
whose laughter filled a room with love.

To my sister Jeanne,
whose love fills a room with laughter.

To my brother Paul,
whose jokes make me laugh.

To my sister Eileen,
whose perseverance inspires me to stay the course.

To my nephews Tom, Michael, Jimmy, Holden, and Joe,
whose smiles and laughter fill my heart with love.

To John,
whose delight in hearing my laugh keeps me light-hearted.

Contents

Acknowledgments

It is so true that it takes a village to raise a book. To do it superbly in record time requires a *nation* of bright, willing, committed people, of which I am blessed to be a part.

Procter & Gamble, thank you for your generous support of *Living with Enthusiasm* and *My Mother, My Friend.* Tricia Montgomery, thank you for asking, "What else?" and saying yes. Debbie Orth, thank you for your organizational skills. Jennifer Dauer, Diane Dietz, and the Crest Team, thank you for your continued support of women's health around the world and your creativity. I love my "Little Mermaid" SpinBrush.

Speaking of Women's Health Team, thank you for opening so many doors for me through the National Speaking of Women's Health Foundation. And thanks to the National Speaking of Women's Health Foundation for making this book a dream come true.

Leslie Charles, thank you for your wondrous gifts of creative editing, friendship, wisdom, generosity, humor, encouragement, and time. Your ideas have added so much to this project and my life. You definitely earned good karma here.

Barbara McNichol, thank you for your amazing copyediting, grammatical gifts, check-in calls, flexibility, and easy-going attitude. You *are* the Grammar Queen.

John Kalpus, thank you for your technology advice, editing time, humor, lunch breaks at Roberto's, and daily check-ins. You kept me sane when my computer crashed and saved me more than a few days when we needed to meet an editing deadline.

Fabulous Readers – Michele Cooney, Holly Herman, John Kalpus, Pamela Maurer, Ellen Osinski, Jennifer Peck, Karen Rowinsky, and Tricia Schreifer, thank you for reading and commenting on the entire manuscript. Your daily feedback was a lifeline for me.

Colleagues and friends – Tanya Abreu, Dan Burrus, Chris Clarke-Epstein, Ken Druck, Annie Duval, Rita Emmett, Roxanne Emmerich, Dan Gardner, Dianne Gardner, Susan Gilbert, Laurel Green, Kathi Ingersoll, Joan Lloyd, Lael Jackson, Deb Kern, Patti Lechmaier, Beca Lewis, Sharon McFarland, Christine Phinney, Mary Rice, Karen Rowinsky, Jana Stanfield, Mark Therrien, Barbara Weiland, and Kathy Zebell, thank you for your brilliance and time. Your interviews, contributions, ideas, friendship, and e-mails and voice mail messages and of love and encouragement enriched this book beyond measure

Caroline Sutton, thank you for your "go ahead," spirit. Laurie Fox, thank you for your friendship, agent-extraordinaire skills, and your always-creative and helpful literary advice. Patrick Miller, thank you for your book production advice. Nancy Greystone, thank you for your media copy eyes!

Lori Prokop, thank you for your creative marketing advice and showing me how to let go of the good so I can embrace the great in record time. Beverly Weurding, thank you for the original title idea of *Living with Enthusiasm* and for being such a great cheerleader for me. You are one of the purest souls I know.

Bob Goodman, thank you for working tirelessly on a very tight timeframe, creating such a readable design, and staying enthusiastic in the process. Laurie Gibson, thank you for being a conscientious soul and a great proofreader. Sharon Tully and the Central Plains Books team, thank you for outstanding service and for making this book beautiful.

HeartMath Friends – Arnold Chalfant, Michele and Michael Cooney, Lynne de Paur, Linda Flores, Michael Michaelson, Laura Fleming, and Doug Franke, and our precious Vivienne, thank you for your weekly prayers and deep heart intelligence. Healing Place Friends – Kathy Konzen, Kim, Renee, Martin, Beverly, and so many others, thank you for your laughter, ideas, and potluck meals!

Peter Rengel, thank you for your permission to reprint your life-changing poem, "Bliss Quota."

Paul and Jan, Eileen, Jeanne and Dick, thank you for letting me share our family stories. Tom, Michael, Jimmy, Holden, and Joe, thank you for being so much fun and always asking how I'm doing. You're extraordinary boys and make me very proud to be your aunt.

Sheri Rush, Debby Borza, Kathi Ingersoll, and all women who have turned grief into action and service, thank you for your courage.

Readers and participants at my programs, thank you for your attention, feedback, laughter, and love. You inspire me, motivate me, and allow me to live my life's purpose. I am blessed!

Creative Spirit, thank you for giving me the people, time, ideas, and connections to create *Living with Enthusiasm*. I am humbled, delighted, and awed by your gifts.

Introduction

It all started with Joyce 20 years ago. Joyce was a high-performing hotel sales rep, active arts supporter, and mother of three teenagers. She was also an image client of mine. Her enthusiasm for life could turn a roomful of pessimists in Pollyannas. Joyce had a huge laugh and was genuinely upbeat, even when her world was crashing down around her. Not that she didn't get upset about things; in fact, her tears and frustration were as big as her laughter. But she seemed able to shake off negative situations and move into positive action in a joyful way faster than anyone I knew.

After several months of observing Joyce at work and home, I wanted that energy and happiness for myself. Not knowing where to start, I asked her one day, full of curiosity, "Joyce, do you always wake up this happy?"

Words burst out of her mouth like an uncorked bottle of champagne. "Mary, I can't wait to jump out of bed every morning and feel my feet hit the ground! And I hate going to sleep at night because there's just so much life to live. Honestly, I can't get enough of it!"

I was stunned. While I loved being an entrepreneur and found my work as an image consultant immensely satisfying, I wasn't hopping out of bed eager to start my day. And I had never heard myself belly laugh like she did, much less laugh out loud without looking to see if someone might think I was acting inappropriately.

Joyce's response left an indelible mark on my heart. Her example set me on a path to capture and bottle that enthusiasm for my life.

Ten years later, my search intensified. My mother's five-month battle with ovarian cancer and subsequent death gave me the opportunity to experience firsthand how short life can be. And it showed me the importance of "going for the gusto" as often as possible...in whatever ways possible...with as many people as possible, now. She reminded me again and again before she died:

Life is short. Life is Precious. Don't wait. Do it now.

Living with Enthusiasm is about going for the gusto *now.* It is filled with inspiring people, powerful lessons, and practical positive strategies that I've discovered on my journey. It will help you take daily action to bring more joy, excitement, delight, passion, love, or whatever you define as enthusiasm into everything you do.

Some days you simply won't feel enthusiastic. You'll even forget you can make more joyful choices in the moment. That's natural. But when you catch yourself out of sync, pick up this book and read even a few sentences. I promise you'll find a story, quote, question, strategy, or activity that will be exactly what you need to shift your funk into fun.

Some people believe enthusiasm is a superficial effort to gain approval, deny reality, mask sadness, or avoid having deep conversations. In some situations, this may be true, but enthusiasm is also an expression of love, joy, and deep caring about a person, idea, thing, or experience. With all the issues we now face – global terrorism, neighborhood violence, increasing weather disasters, environmental illness, and just day-to-day stress, I believe the world needs *all* of our enthusiasm, optimism, ideas, and compassionate support.

What's the 21-Day Smile Diet?

For the past year, I've had the privilege of speaking around the country for Speaking of Women's Health events on the topic of "Brighten Up and Smile: Your Self-Esteem, Your Smile, and Your Health," sponsored by Procter & Gamble's Crest. When preparing for that program, I was amazed to find a huge body of research on the power of a smile. A smile impacts your self-confidence, health, relationships, success, and overall zest for living. A smile *really can* change your life.

The **21-Day Smile Diet** idea came to me in a creative flash following a conversation with Laurel Green at a Speaking of Women's Health event in

Kansas City, Missouri. Laurel is a women's health hospital administrator and a wife, mother, and volunteer. She told me about her system for losing 50 pounds, and it inspired me tremendously. She didn't go on a formal diet, yet still her weight melted off over a year's time. She attributes this to three actions she took: (1) eating a little less every day, (2) exercising a little more every day, (3) and most importantly, committing to doing a fun activity every day – just for herself. After we talked, I could not get out of my head the idea of losing weight through a *daily commitment* of fun.

On the plane home to San Diego, I started comparing the contradiction of the words "diet" and "fun." If the two were human beings, their relationship would never last. This idea made me laugh. Out of the blue popped the words "Smile Diet." The more I thought about it, the more I realized this could be a great format for living with enthusiasm.

From all of my years in leading seminars on stress management and personal change, I knew that it took a minimum of 21 days to make or break a habit. I also knew that people function best when they have a system to follow that also allows for fun. Yes! A **21-Day Smile Diet** was exactly what was needed to make enthusiasm a regular part of anyone's life.

Whether or not weight loss is your goal, the **21-Day Smile Diet** format feeds and nourishes your body, mind, spirit, heart, and soul. As you begin doing more things for yourself that feel good, the unhealthy behaviors begin to fall away. This diet is fun and doesn't require denying yourself chocolate! It is a system to help you create more energy and delight in your daily life, not just on vacations or when the Universe surprises you out of the blue. I know from firsthand experience that it will increase your zest for life and give you a program you can follow forever.

What's the Best Way to Use This Book?

Living with Enthusiasm is organized into 21 readings within five chapters that cover what enthusiasm is, why enthusiasm is important, characteristics of enthusiastic people, the secret to daily enthusiasm, and how to keep enthusiasm alive during challenging times.

You'll learn about the latest research on enthusiasm and how it impacts workplace hiring decisions, healing, and relationships. You'll be coached on how to appreciate and celebrate yourself more often without guilt. And you'll discover principles that give yourself permission to say "no" to the good and "yes" to the great.

Starting with Day 1, you'll greet each day with a question, inspiring quotations, and life-changing stories about people who have discovered how to create and sustain enthusiasm in their lives. At the end of each day, there will be an action step for you to take that will increase your pleasure, additional tips to help you create more enthusiasm, and questions to ask yourself that will enhance your self-awareness. I'll encourage you to share your renewed passion with others. If you wish to deepen your knowledge of a particular topic, go to the resource section at the end of book, which includes web sites, books, magazines, movies, and music.

I invite you to share this unique and personal program with a friend or a group of friends or extended family. Encourage everyone to commit to the program for the full 21 days for the greatest benefit. Or extend the benefits and use the book for 21 weeks, focusing on one day's information for a week at a time. Do a weekly phone call with a friend or get your group together once a week for reinforcement. Or just let your intuition guide you. Browse the Table of Contents or open to any page for inspiration and ideas that might put more enthusiasm into your life.

Whatever you do, remember: This journey is about adding more joy, excitement, delight, passion, and love into everything you do. Let your enthusiasm lead the way and share your results with as many people as possible. As my friend Jana Stanfield writes and sings so beautifully, "The world needs all the good that you can do."

I would love to hear from you along the way and invite you to e-mail me at mary@marymarcdante.com.

Watch for miracles. They are on their way.

Enthusiastically,

Mary Marcdante
January 2003

Chapter One

What is Enthusiasm?

Meet Rose Bradley. Spry like an elf. Five feet tall, silver ponytail down to the middle of her back. Dressed in a fluorescent orange, lime green, and brown paisley polyester blouse, with matching brown polyester vested pantsuit and sensible black Reebok running shoes. Black reading glasses perched on the tip of her nose. It's 1996 and Rose is in my audience, one of 500 people gathered to hear me speak on creating a fulfilling life.

I'm in the midst of talking to the audience about the importance of vision and mission. I tell them about the Blue Rinse Nursing Home and Café, an idea I dreamed up with two speaker friends, Rox and Chris, so we'd all be guaranteed at least an audience of two to listen to our stories when we got old. I ask audience members to imagine they are 80 years old and applying for admittance to the Blue Rinse.

"The only way you can be accepted to the Blue Rinse," I say, "is if you have at least one great adventure between now and the time you apply to the Blue Rinse that is worthy of a standing ovation. That way, those of us who are already there will be guaranteed a little exercise beyond rocking in our chairs. And you'll live at least one of those dreams we all talk about."

I give them a few minutes to reflect on their visions. When I ask if anyone wants to share their adventures with the group, Rose jumps out of her seat in the front row, comes running up to the stage, and asks for the microphone. She looks so excited I can't resist her, even though it goes against everything I've learned as a speaker about controlling a room.

As she speaks into the microphone, I am shocked by her voice. It belies her tiny appearance. It is deep and gravelly and strong like a man's.

She bellows, "My name's Rose Bradley. My nickname's 'The General.' I'm in my 79th year now. You say you want everyone to have a big adventure by the time they turn 80 at this Blue Rinse Nursing Home and Café. Well, when I was younger, I used to tease everybody and tell 'em I was going to be the first pregnant woman on the moon. With the way technology's going, I may just make it."

She went on to say, "My vision for the future when I turn 80 next year is to buy a franchise of the Blue Rinse Nursing Home and Café on the moon. Would you let me in?"

Rose's enthusiasm for living at age 79 had an entire ballroom of 500 people laughing to tears. When they recovered, they jumped out of their seats and gave her a standing ovation.

Enthusiasm isn't about how old you are or how tall you are or what you do for a living. It's not about how loud you are, how much money you have, or what kind of car you drive. Enthusiasm is about how willing you are to be your biggest, brightest self in the world. It's about sharing with the world what makes you laugh, what delights you, what you're passionate about, and whom you love. And more importantly, sharing that love with yourself.

For some, enthusiasm is big and bold and out-front like Rose Bradley or your brother who tells great jokes or your co-worker who has the next great idea that will change the world. For others, it's a much quieter expression – a smile, a sparkle in the eyes, a hand reaching out to offer support. Enthusiasm has many faces. Our journey together in this book will help you discover your unique expressions of enthusiasm so you can bring them to the table of life more often and with greater ease.

Discover Your Unique Expressions of Enthusiasm

To add more enthusiasm to your life, start by doing a baseline measurement. This will identify what enthusiasm looks like to you and how it manifests itself in you now. At the end of the book, we'll take another look to see what's changed and by how much. Then we'll help you celebrate your growth.

The word "enthusiasm" comes from the Greek word "enthousiasmos," which means "to be inspired." This originated from "entheos," which is the combination of "en" (in) plus "theos" (god). Webster's Dictionary includes three meanings: belief in the revelations of the Holy Spirit; a strong feeling of excitement; something inspiring passion. Roget's Thesaurus lists more than 100 different words to describe enthusiasm:

Dynamism, physical energy, dynamic energy, dynamic, dynamics, pressure, force, impetus, energy, intensity, high pressure, strength, dash, élan, pizzazz, impetuosity, haste, exertion, effort, labor, fervor, enthusiasm, vigor, gusto, relish, zest, zest for life, zestfulness, joy, liveliness, spirit, vim, vim and vigor, vitality, zing, zip, éclat, fire, mettle, pluck, nerve, guts, courage, gumption, spunk, verve, snap, pep, drive, go, get up and go, enterprise, initiative, undertaking, vehemence, violence, aggressiveness, oomph, thrust, push, kick, punch, attack, grip, bite, teeth, backbone, determination, resolution, endurance, grit, stamina, stick-to-it-iveness, virility, vitality, live wire, spark, spitfire, dynamo, dynamite, quicksilver, rocket, jet, display of energy, spurt, show of force, demonstration, intimidation.

What's your definition of enthusiasm? Write down a few of the words from above that call to you. Or create your own definition that best describes enthusiasm to you.

Different Types of Enthusiasm

Enthusiasm operates on many levels. At its simplest there is "childlike" enthusiasm, which is light-hearted and innocent; its only purpose is to delight in the moment. At its most profound, there is enthusiasm that comes from the desire to serve humanity, and to forward a belief or cause, which ultimately makes a positive difference in the world. At its most charming or irritating, depending on the personality, is a huckster-type display of "fake" enthusiasm. While containing a lot of energy, it does not ultimately feed our spirit. What is common to all expressions of genuine enthusiasm is that they are heartfelt and honest, and they uplift our soul and sustain our spirit.

What Creates Enthusiasm?

What generates enthusiasm are many positive qualities, including optimism, appreciation, healthy humor, compassion, joy, happiness, love, wonder, curiosity, hope, purpose, courage, connection, and many others that we'll explore throughout the next 21 days. As you answer the question below, keep the above qualities in mind.

Who is one of the most genuinely enthusiastic people you know? What makes that person appear that way? How does he or she act?

Once you have a basic definition of enthusiasm and what it looks like, it helps to know how you personally experience enthusiasm. So next, describe a situation in which you've shown enthusiasm. If you can't think of a time right now, go back and read the words above. Does anything pop out? If not, keep reading and come back to this after your mind has had some time to warm up. I promise you that a deep well of enthusiasm resides within you. It just needs time and permission to wake up, and then WOW! You'll be bursting with ideas and opportunities to share your spirit every day.

Where were you?

What were you doing?

Who was with you?

What were you thinking?

Where did you feel enthusiasm in your body?

Notice how you're feeling right now after spending time thinking about and writing out your positive experiences. It feels good, doesn't it? How often do you do this on a daily basis? I'm guessing, like most people you'd answer, "Not often enough." It sounds like a cliché but it's so true: The more you do it, the more you get it.

> *One of the things I think we need is to love people with enthusiasm. The years may wrinkle your skin, but a lack of enthusiasm wrinkles your soul.*
> – Ruth Cleveland

Create Your Enthusiasm Benchmark

To create your benchmark, let's look at how you perceive yourself. Circle your best answers to the next three questions.

On a scale of 1–5, how enthusiastic are you?

1 2 3 4 5

Depressed — Depends on situation — Pretty Up — Off the charts

On a scale of 1–5, if your family, three closest friends, and co-workers got together and did a group rating, how would they rate your level of enthusiasm?

1 2 3 4 5

Depressed — Depends on situation — Pretty Up — Off the charts

On a scale of 1–5, where would you like to be?

1 2 3 4 5

Depressed — Depends on situation — Pretty Up — Off the charts

How did you do? Are you where you want to be? If so, congratulations. By reading the rest of this book, you'll continue to keep yourself, as my mother loved to say, "full of the dickens," and be ready to share these ideas with others who may need them.

If you want more enthusiasm, you've come to the right place. We're going to have such a good time together that you'll naturally find yourself feeling more excited about your life day by day. By the end of these 21 days together, you'll want to do it all over again and share it with friends.

Three Tips to Start Your Journey

Whatever your level of enthusiasm is, you can increase it. To start your journey:

- Pay attention to when you feel enthusiastic and do more of whatever you're doing.
- Notice when you feel negative emotions or low energy, acknowledge those feelings to yourself (this is important; recognition = release), then choose a new thought or action that moves you toward more enthusiasm.
- Watch others who are enthusiastic and ask them how they stay energized.

As we progress using the **21-Day Smile Diet** to strengthen your enthusiasm muscle, I'll help you identify your thoughts and actions that create and sustain enthusiasm uniquely for you. For the purposes of fun and learning, we'll start each day with a question and four possible responses. (Keep a pen handy. I encourage you to write in this book and make it your own.) You may or may not find yourself in these answers; more importantly, just notice which response you most identify with and use it as a springboard for self-discovery. The remainder of the day's ideas and suggestions will help fill in the blanks. By the time you reach Day 21, your mind, body, and spirit will know truly, passionately, and deeply what enthusiasm is. By then, you'll have a gym full of tips and strategies to choose from to keep your energy high and your heart happy.

> *If you want to keep happy and healthy, try being an "inverse paranoid." An "inverse paranoid" is someone who thinks everyone is out to make him happy!*
>
> —Rich Bimler

Day 1

The 21-Day Smile Diet

How often do you find yourself smiling during the day?

a. What's to smile for? The world's such a mess. Besides, I heard it takes 17 muscles to smile and 43 to frown. I hate to exercise so the more muscles I can use without much effort, the better.

b. Once. At exactly five o'clock p.m. every Monday through Friday and twice on the second and fourth Fridays...when I get my paycheck.

c. I've never thought about it. Maybe 10–20 times a day. But when I smile, I hardly ever show my teeth because they're not perfect and I can't afford to get them fixed.

d. My life is a smile! I hunt for smiles. Everywhere I look, there's something to smile about no matter what's going on in my life.

~ ~ ~ ~ ~ ~ ~ ~ ~ ~

Please humor me if you would, for 16 seconds. This will be fun, I promise.

Put a smile on your face. Now make it bigger. Now smile like the Cheshire Cat in *Alice in Wonderland* – ear to ear. Keep holding your smile and now breathe in deeply through your nose. Keep holding the smile and now let out your breath. Repeat twice more (your brain learns with repetition of threes).

Great job! Now look around and see if people are watching you. If they are, make a big smile again, hold it, raise your eyebrows, and then wave to them. If they engage you, feel free to share what you're doing with them and have a good laugh together. When you're finished, I invite you back to keep reading. If they don't respond or weren't watching, just keep reading and enjoying the burst of feel-good chemicals – endorphins – your brain just sent to your body.

Consider the above request and breathing exercise as your introduction to Enthusiasm 101. Mind, body, and breath are the essence of enthusiasm. If you are already an enthusiastic or active person, just like an Olympic athlete, think of the previous exercise as a warm-up for going for the "gold-medal" life.

In this **21-Day Smile Diet**, we'll explore different ways you can jump-start your enthusiasm day-by-day, keep yourself (and others) smiling, and put your system in what research scientist Mihali Csikszentmihalyi calls a "state of flow."

On Day 1, we're focusing on one of the most readily available and powerful enthusiasm generators in existence – your smile.

Say Cheese

A smile is the most universally recognized and understood gesture every culture understands and 99.9 percent of the population enjoys giving and receiving. We can identify a smile more easily than any other expression, even from a distance of up to 300 feet. We smile when we feel good, when we see someone we love, when we reach a long-awaited goal, when we're embarrassed, and when we need to mask anger we can't appropriately express at the moment. We even smile on cue when anyone with a camera calls out, "Say cheese."

Different Types of Smiles

University of California at San Francisco researcher Paul Ekman and his colleagues identified 19 different types of smiles. Categorized into two basic categories, polite "social" smiles engage only mouth muscles, and genuine, happy "felt" smiles activate muscles on both sides of the mouth and around the eyes. Felt smiles light up the left frontal cortex of the brain where pleasure is registered.

University of California at Berkeley psychologists Dacher Keltner and Lee Ann Harker identified six basic types of smiles to express feelings. The last three turn on the enthusiasm switch. They are:

- POLITE Smile: We turn up both corners of our lips, but there's no engagement with our eyes. We give this smile to strangers.
- ASYMMETRICAL Smile: We raise one side of our lips higher than the other. This is also referred to as a fake smile.
- EMBARRASSED Smile: We bend our heads forward a little, look away or down, and press our lips together when we smile. It's used when we have made a mistake, overstepped our limits, or been caught doing something against the norm.
- GENUINE Smile: Our lips raise up and part, our teeth may even show. Our eyes light up and crow's feet (tiny wrinkles that do have a grander purpose!) appear on our skin around the edges of our eyes. A muscle under our eyes also lifts up. (For some people, it's the best and only exercise they get all day!) It's also known as the "Duchenne Smile," named after an 18th century French neurologist who first reported on "smiles of the will" and "smiles of the heart."
- LOVING Smile: We tilt our heads toward others while we're doing the GENUINE smile.
- SYNCHRONIZED Smile: We do the GENUINE, LOVING smile and add a forward-leaning body movement toward the recipient, showing that we're on the same wavelength.

Physiologically and emotionally, a smile tells our brains that we are safe, that we fit in (or want to fit in), and that we can relax. When we smile at others, it sends a message of trust and goodwill. Consequently, we're seen as open and approachable.

Chances are you've rarely given thought to the impact of your smile on your energy level, health, success, or relationships. You may have been aware of your "grin factor" if you were a shy, serious child prodded by your parents to smile for the neighbors. Or, as a teen, if you had a crush on someone and practiced your smile in the mirror while having an imaginary conversation. Or, more seriously, if you are self-conscious about your teeth or you feel depressed and just can't seem to find your smile at all.

Smiles are a sign of good health and happiness. Keltner's research at the University of California at Berkeley also showed that practicing the smiles of enthusiasm – the genuine smile, the loving smile, and the synchronized smile – on a regular basis will positively impact how you feel and perform in life. Keltner reviewed the lives of 100 women over a 30-year period after graduation from Mills College. He found that women who had the most intense smiles in their high school photos were married sooner, stayed married longer, and were happier in their lives than those who smiled with less intensity.

By their 50s, the women with the bigger smiles were 20 percent more likely to be happily married, 20 percent less likely to have serious tension in their lives, and 27 percent more likely to have a strong sense of well-being.

We don't usually think about the value of our smiles until we've lost them.

– Mary Marcdante

The Power of Your Smile

Imagine that you're like a woman I met named Linda: homeless, without a job, on welfare with two young children. You've been living in a domestic violence shelter for three weeks, hiding from an angry, abusive spouse who knocked out four of your front teeth. Your self-esteem is at an all-time low and the last thing you want to do is put a smile on your face. Yet a smile is the very thing you most need from yourself and from others to help you start putting your life back together again.

Now imagine a compassionate volunteer who smiles at you without judgment and offers you an enthusiastic hug every morning. Soon, you're beginning to feel a smile creep back on your face and thinking that you maybe you can make it. Never underestimate the power of your smile and energy to change another person's life. Thanks to programs like Francie Pepper's Safe House in Cincinnati and family shelters across the country, women like Linda can get the help they need to rebuild their smiles and their lives.

Whether our lives have been torn apart like Linda's or we're fortunate enough to say, "There but for the grace of God go I," how *do* we keep healthy and enthusiastic smiles on our faces on a daily basis?

I spent two and a half years in college studying dental hygiene. At my first class clinic, I fainted. When I came to, I immediately realized I was happier carving wax teeth than cleaning real teeth. So I withdrew from the dental program and enrolled in art school. But the lessons I learned about the importance of oral health stay with me to this day:

- Love your dental hygienist
- Visit your dentist once, preferably twice a year
- Don't smoke (reach for floss instead!)
- Brush and floss twice a day
- And two new suggestions that make all the difference in the size of your smile:
  - Whiten your teeth. (Crest has these very cool Whitestrips you can get at the grocery store or drug store.)
  - Use a power brush because you'll brush better and longer. (I love my Crest "Little Mermaid" SpinBrush and give them as birthday gifts to friends!)

Create Your Own Personal Smile Ritual

When comedienne Carol Burnett sang her closing song to the audience on her weekly television show, she ended it with a smile and a tug on her left earlobe. This ritual signaled to her grandmother Nanny that all was right with the world.

I have a smiling ritual I do when I'm shopping. Whether it's the grocery store, department store, restaurant, dry cleaner, office supply store, or gas station, I enjoy getting checked out (no, not that kind of "checked out," although the older I get, the more appealing that sounds). When it's my turn, I send out a big smile and attempt to make eye contact with the checkout person. Sometimes we become fast friends, discussing the latest gossip on the cover of the *National Enquirer* or *The Globe.* Other times, it takes several seconds for me to connect with them because they're so focused on their tasks.

There's a deeper reason we're not connecting. When I started talking with frontline people, I learned that many of them feel undervalued and unappreciated. They work long hours for low wages. They smile a lot, say hello, and in return they often get complaints or disinterest from customers. Having worked during my high school and college days as a cashier at Shore-Vu Grocery Store, a waitress at the Pig'n Whistle, and a babysitter for three siblings and 24 neighbor children, I can identify with them. I'm guessing you can, too.

It's easy to be enthusiastic and smiling when people are in a good mood or feel kind and helpful. You and I both know it's another story when someone's cranky or rude.

> *Every time you smile at someone, it is an action of love, a gift to that person, a beautiful thing.*
>
> – Mother Teresa

I frequent a gas station that employs a dour-looking, older service attendant. It appears that life has not been kind to him. I first noticed him one day when the pumps were broken and customers had to go into the office to pay for gas. When I handed this curmudgeon my credit card, I smiled as I normally did. He didn't smile back. Irritated, I thought, "Who does he think he is? I'm paying him. He ought to be friendlier, considering the prices we pay here." I left feeling annoyed.

The following week I went back, hoping for a different attendant. No such luck. There he was, as usual, looking distant and grumpy. I pumped my gas and used the credit card machine at the gas pump to pay my bill. My evil twin was on my left shoulder, feeding me sarcastic one-liners just in case he looked my way. But Mother Teresa was sitting on the right shoulder and she won. As I was leaving, I forced a penitent smile and waved to him. Lucky me: I caught his attention and received a "Make my day" stare. My self-esteem was beginning to get involved. This man must be on downers! I haven't done anything to him, I thought. I smiled even bigger – like a chimpanzee, almost glaring. Still no facial movement from him. Not even a muscle twitch. What was wrong with this guy?!

Ready to find another gas station but sensing Mother T smiling at me from above, I decided to give it one more try. I was on a mission. I vowed to myself that, for the benefit of humanity, I would somehow find a way to make him smile before I left the station the next time.

If you would like to spoil the day for a grouch, give him a smile.

– Anonymous

D-Day arrived a week later. I pumped my gas. As I walked toward the glass-plated window and wide open door, I focused a laser-beam "I know there's something good in you somewhere down there" smile on him. No deal. Nothing. Nada. Zip. "This guy is a tough cookie," I thought.

Plan B. As he put his hand out for my credit card, I was prepared. I imagined being Julia Roberts. With a full-on smile, I started to move the card toward his hand and just as his fingers went to grab it, I pulled the card back. I said, "I'll bet you have a great smile. I'll give you my card if you give me a smile." I fully expected him to crack a smile, maybe even chuckle a bit, so I was unprepared for what he said in the most downtrodden, flat voice and broken English: "Ma'am, if I smile at you, there's a real good chance you're going to misinterpret my smile and I could end up with a lawsuit for appearing to solicit your services. That's why I don't smile. I am not in my own country and life is hard here. I want to keep my job."

My heart ached for him, for me, for the world, for all the times we hesitate to offer our humanity out of resentment, anger, fear of litigation, violence, rape, or even simple miscommunication. "I understand," I said, feeling tears well up. Embarrassed, I fumbled for a moment and then responded. "Thank you for being so honest. I'm sorry it's so hard for you. I appreciate all that you do." I smiled. And of all things, he smiled back.

There are hundreds of languages in the world, but a smile speaks them all.

– Anonymous

Now, every time I go into the gas station and finish pumping my gas, as I drive past the open door, I teasingly take my index finger, push up the left corner of my lips, and the right corner follows. From behind the glass-plated window, a smile beams back. Compassion and understanding are high-octane fuels that keep the engine of enthusiasm running at an optimal level and deliver a smile 99 percent of the time.

Turn Your Smile into a Joy Machine

Someone needs your smile today. When you're out in the world in the next 24 hours, turn your smile into a joy machine. Look for someone whose services you use that could benefit from an ear tug, a kind word, an extra second of eye contact, understanding, or your biggest smile.

> *Nobody needs a smile so much as the one who has none to give.*
> *So get used to smiling heart-warming smiles,*
> *and you will spread sunshine in a sometimes-dreary world.*
>
> – Lawrence G. Lovasik

Today's Action Step

Give yourself a big smile in every mirror or window reflection you see yourself in. If you're a really extroverted person, wave back. People will wonder what you're up to, and most will smile and shake their heads. You might just make their day.

Tips for Creating More Enthusiasm

- ❑ Keep a small spiral notebook with you for a day, or get a counter and click the number of smiles you make in a day. Aim for 50 *genuine* smiles.
- ❑ See how long you can hold a smile and eye contact with another person before you start laughing or have to look away. Work up to one minute.
- ❑ Notice other people's smiles, even if they're off in the distance, and smile along with them to get in on the good feelings. Practice random acts of smiling.

- ❑ Study your smile in the mirror. Spend a few minutes trying different smiles and then give yourself a genuine smile and hold it for 16 seconds.
- ❑ Get involved in National Smile Week in August to promote dental health or participate in World Smile Day on October 4, which was started by Harvey Ball, who created the "Smiley Face." (A simple drawing of a smiling face on a yellow background.) Follow his motto: "Do something kind. Make one person smile."

Questions to Ask Yourself

- How many times did you smile yesterday?
- Who and what make you smile? List at least 10 people and things.
- What was going on during a recent time when your smile made a big difference to someone else?
- When has someone's smile healed a hurt or dramatically affected your life? Who was that person?
- Who are three service people you frequently see who could use an extra smile and a kind word from you?

Day 2

Oh, What a Beautiful Morning

Do you wake up with a smile on your face?

a. No, but my dog does.

b. My face wakes up in park. I need all the help I can get.

c. Once in a while, if I've had a good dream or I'm excited about something I'll be doing that day.

d. I love mornings. As soon as I know I'm awake, I choose to smile as big as I can, take a deep breath, and say a prayer, "Thank you for another day."

~ ~ ~ ~ ~ ~ ~ ~ ~ ~ ~

"Oh, what a beautiful morning. Oh, what a beautiful day. I've got a wonderful feeling, everything's going my way." What does it take for you to be able to agree with the words of this classic song? For some, it's our fake-it-til-you-make-it attitude. For other grin-and-bear-it types, it's our morning cup of coffee or a hot shower. And for those who are fortunate to be "merry in the morning," it's just the way our brains are wired. Or is it?

How you wake up in the morning matters. Stephen F. Covey, the author of the perennially popular *Seven Habits of Highly Effective People*, has a great rule to make your day an enthusiastic one: Start with the end in mind. How do you want to feel when you wake up in the morning, and what actions do you need to take to make it a great day? After all, it's your decision!

Kate, a mother of three teenage boys, rises before dawn, grateful to spend an hour in her favorite Queen Anne chair, praying and writing in her journal. Leslie sets two alarms, one for 5:45 a.m. and the other for 6:05

a.m. This lets her spend 20 minutes luxuriating in a dreamlike, cozy mind-space, snuggling in the warmth of her down comforter and petting her purring cat before her busy day begins. Carrie jumps out of bed before the alarm clock goes off, dresses in sweats, sprints into her teenage daughter's room, wakes her with a kiss on the forehead, then dashes off for a morning run with two friends while humming her favorite morning mantra, "Zippity Do Dah." Jennifer hits the alarm button six times in 18 minutes while her annoyed husband lies next to her contemplating divorce. She drags herself out of bed, shuffles to the kitchen, turns on the coffee pot, collects the paper at the back door, and yells to the kids to get up.

Which of these women is destined to have the most stressful day? Which will best cope with whatever the day brings? It doesn't take a rocket scientist to determine that certain actions support our well-being and others undermine it. Our challenge is to act on the choices we know will help make it a great day.

Take a look at your morning routine and explore these questions:

> How did you wake up as a child? What is one of your favorite childhood morning memories? (If you can't remember, or didn't have one, create a new ritual.)
>
> Does the way you start your day support you in having a great day? What's getting in your way? What's the best thing you do for yourself in the morning?
>
> What one action could you change or create that would help you have a better day?

Rise and Shine, Kids! The World is Waiting for You

From as early as I can remember until I left home for college at 17, every weekday morning at 6 a.m. my father, an architect and former U.S. Marine Corp. private, would march up the 22 stairs to the second floor. In his booming baritone voice, he'd stop at the top, shout his morning revelry, "Rise and shine, kids! The world is waiting for you," and march back down. If there was no movement by 6:30 (which was almost every day, the older we got), we'd hear his heavy footsteps pounding up the stairs again. By the time he reached the 17th stair, I would scramble out of bed to avoid his lecture that "the early bird gets the worm," and hustle to beat my three siblings to the bathroom.

Chocolate Milk, Long Johns, and Icicles

My favorite morning memory was a summer Saturday when I was nine. In those days, milkmen still delivered milk, butter, and eggs early in the morning and television hadn't arrived on the scene at our house yet. My three siblings and I were up before Dad, rushing to the magical milk chute in the back hall to add an extra bottle of chocolate milk to the milkman's order before he arrived. That day we gulped Golden Guernsey chocolate milk right from the bottle while still in our pajamas, passing it between each other until it was gone. Heaven! But it gets even better. We got dressed and woke up Dad, who drove us over to Pete's Bakery to choose our favorite doughnuts (long john with icing for me) and frozen "icicle" (cherry or lime), which we ate in the car on the ride home. When we arrived back home, my mother had coffee waiting for my father. He gave her a kiss, prepared her favorite doughnut – a "butter longhorn" (a long, skinny croissant in the shape of a horn) slathered with Jiffy peanut butter – and sat with her to plan our family's day.

They say old habits die hard and for me that is true. To this day, one of my favorite things is to hear someone greet me in the morning. Only now, it's the paws of my cat standing on my chest meowing for breakfast or the first telemarketer of the day saying "Have a nice day." I still love long johns but so much sweetness makes my teeth ache. Instead, I treat myself to a chai tea and Starbuck's almond biscotti on Saturday mornings. For my sister Jeanne, it's still chocolate milk she loves – only now, for her birthday, she asks her husband or sons to serve it to her in her favorite champagne glass.

What is one of your favorite childhood morning memories or rituals?

____

____

Are you still doing any of these rituals? If not, what aspect of that childhood morning ritual would be fun or meaningful to incorporate into your life now?

____

____

Commit to One Morning Ritual

Mornings can be stressful. If you're trying to get a family out the door for school, running a business from your home, caring for elderly parents or even neighbors who need to be looked in on, life can distract you from your own morning self-care. Whatever your routine looks like, decide that you will commit to one morning ritual that enhances your day, then do it *no matter what.* Your commitment to yourself is one of the core elements that feeds enthusiasm. And if you keep on giving to others without attending to yourself, you may end up burned out or resentful.

If time is an issue, which it is for most of us, here are two smile strategies you can complete in five minutes or less: the 16-Second Smile and the Smiling-Thank You Meditation. I guarantee doing them will help your day go more smoothly. If all you learn and practice from this book are these two techniques, you will change your life forever.

Start every day with a smile and get it over with.

– W.C. Fields

Wake up with a 16-Second Smile

These two smile strategies are my favorites-of-all-times. They have improved my attitude dramatically and have skyrocketed my energy level, especially when I wake up feeling blue. They have also received the most fan mail from participants in my programs. These two techniques take less than a minute to do and if you do them for up to 15 minutes, you will feel a *significant* positive change immediately, including a euphoric tingling in your body.

SMILE STRATEGY 1: 16-Second Smile: At the moment you are aware of being awake, smile for 16 seconds, just as I suggested you do at the beginning of Day 1. Make that smile as genuine as possible – activate the eye crinkles and slowly breathe in. Notice how good it feels to smile. As you let your breath out, keep smiling and imagine those endorphins traveling all through you.

SMILE STRATEGY 2: Smiling-Thank You Meditation: Turn that 16-second smile into a one-to-five-minute meditation. As you're smiling, say the words, "Thank you," over and over again as a mantra. You may notice images of loved ones or pleasant memories forming in your mind. Enjoy them. Or purposefully call up positive images, memories, or upcoming events that will enhance the experience and boost your energy while releasing stress.

Don't limit yourself to doing these two smile strategies only when you wake up. I incorporate both of them into my day and whenever I catch myself in a negative thought, I shift to a long smile and get an instant burst of energy.

Breakfast at the Enthusiasm Café

Do people know how to fuel their bodies for maximum energy in the morning? If surveys are any indication of the population's awareness, the answer is: sort of. According to a *U.S. News and World Report* study, 67 percent of Americans eat cereal for breakfast, 36 percent eat toast or bagels, and 9 percent prefer pancakes, sausages, and waffles. (Total percentage is more than 100 percent because some cereal eaters also eat toast at the same time.) You'll keep your brain happier by starting off with a banana or other piece of fresh fruit followed by whole-grain low-sugar cereal along with low-fat dairy, soy, or rice milk. And if you really want to push the envelope, try lunch for breakfast or eat like I do – either vegetable stew or broccoli cereal (steamed broccoli that I puree and sweeten with stevia – a natural sweetener you can get at the health foods store). It might sound unappetizing, but once you realize how focused, alert, and light you feel all morning because of it, you'll be a convert.

To keep your brain nourished and give you quick and steady energy throughout the day, here are four tips from nutritionist Zonya Foco, author of *Lickety-Split Meals for Health Conscious People on the Go!*

- Eat several (2–4) fresh fruits per day, starting early in the day.
- Eat lots of deeply colored vegetables, favoring carrots, sweet potatoes, broccoli, green and red peppers, cauliflower, cabbage, spinach, and kale. These build the blood with nutrients that energize cells.
- Take moderate dosages of multi-vitamin and mineral supplements for nutrition insurance, and take them consistently.
- Hydrate! Start the moment you get up in the morning because you're always a little dehydrated upon rising. If eight glasses of water a day makes you float, you may only need three or so. (Having clear urine is a good indicator that you're drinking enough.)

And while you're at it, enjoy your breakfast with the television off. Do you really want all that violence starting your day? Wait until your body has had a chance to wake up peacefully before you bombard your senses with the latest tragedy of the day.

Limit Your News to Once a Day in the Middle of the Day

Integrative medicine expert Dr. Andrew Weil, author of *Eight Weeks to Optimum Health: A Proven Program for Taking Full Advantage of Your Body's Natural Healing Power*, says to limit taking in the news to once a day in the middle of the day and in printed form rather than on television. The important news will greet you on the radio as you drive to work, and your digestive system will be grateful. We'll talk more about focusing on sensory pleasures on Day 6. For now, simply spend more time smiling in between your bites of whole grain toast. Or slow down and smile when you're inhaling the smells of your fresh vegetable soup.

Once you've finished breakfast and are ready to fly out the door, here's the last thing to do before you leave: Find a mirror, put a big genuine smile on your face, and say out loud to yourself, "You are going to have an amazing day today!" Just watch. You will.

> *Seize the moment. Remember all those women on the* Titanic *who waved off the dessert cart.*
>
> – Erma Bombeck

Today's Action Step

Practice the 16-Second Smile as often as you can think of it today. Smile before each meal and when you finish. Smile before you dial the phone. Commit to waking every day for the next 21 days with a smile on your face.

Tips for Creating More Enthusiasm

- ❑ Pet or brush your cat or dog for one minute.
- ❑ Keep a vial of essential oils on your bedside table and wake up to rose, lavender, or geranium scents.
- ❑ Kiss your spouse or children good morning before you use the bathroom.
- ❑ Wake up to a CD of soothing music rather than blaring radio talk or news.
- ❑ Do a walking meditation around the block or through your home before going to work. Or create a labyrinth in your backyard and walk in it for your meditation.

Questions to Ask Yourself

- What's one of the most fun or pleasant memories you have of waking up in the morning?
- What phrase, prayer, or quote could you say that would start your day on a light note?
- What's the very first thing you do after you get out of bed in the morning?

- What one action could you eliminate that would cause less stress in the morning?
- What one action could you change or add that would make it more fun to get up?
  - Fun slippers?
  - A more colorful robe?
  - Affirmations posted on the bathroom mirror ("Life is a gift and I feel great!")?
  - Love notes to your family (and yourself) on the toilet seat, inside the refrigerator, or in their lunch bags?

Chapter Two

Why Is Enthusiasm Important To You?

Enthusiasm, however you define it, is at the core of all success. Whether you're hoping to achieve a big dream, heal your body, find peace of mind, influence a client to choose your product, push for a promotion, derive more pleasure from your community or church, or have deeper committed relationships with those you love, enthusiasm can help. In the next five days, we'll look at fascinating research on why creating and sustaining more enthusiasm in your life is so valuable. Even if you're tempted to pass up this section because you're not a research kind of person, stick with it. Each day you'll learn about the latest research that includes real people with challenges like yours and mine, complete with solutions.

If you've ever been in a "why bother?" mood about anything in your life, stop and answer that question for yourself with sincerity. Know why it's important to open your valve and tap into the ever-present, free, and flowing stream of enthusiasm. It can help you shift your mood and propel you into positive action faster.

Perhaps you remember when Richard Carlson's best-selling book, *Don't Sweat the Small Stuff,* was released. I do. I wish I'd written it! It offers simple, effective strategies that we often overlook in this busy, sometimes crazy-making world we live in that can make a big difference in our daily lives. Carlson told us, "Don't sweat the small stuff...and it's all small stuff." We believed him, and had every reason to do so, until September 11.

Following September 11, people began to ask Carlson and *all* inspirational leaders, "How can we get through this? Your techniques are great for little stuff but what about the big stuff? How do we cope with tragedy? Will we ever laugh again?"

The answer, as you know, is, "Yes. In time." What we know from research and experience is that pain can be lessened and healing speeded up when we make time every day for hopeful, joyful thinking and doing. And in his newest book, *What About the Big Stuff?,* Carlson writes:

> I believe it's important to maintain a sense of humor and perspective. I say this not to minimize the severity of anything we must deal with as human beings, but as a way through it. When you look around at all the people going through big things, you'll quickly notice that those who fare best are the ones who somehow manage to keep their perspective and sense of humor. At times it's hard to see how they do it – but they do, and it's genuine. Part of it is that the best antidote to pain is joy. The more we appreciate and experience joy, the better able we are to balance the pain and keep things in perspective.

Thank you, Dr. Carlson. When I first considered writing this book, I worried that after September 11, a book on enthusiasm would be an insult to the tragedy that had occurred. I was concerned that this project may seem too trite to write about. In the days following the horrific tragedy, I wondered how to best respond – as you probably did. The initial outpouring of support, encouragement, prayers, compassion, and financial contributions from people around the world was beyond belief. By comparison, would a book on living with enthusiasm be accepted as a meaningful contribution?

I didn't have to wonder very long. On September 13, 2001, I was scheduled to give a speech in San Diego to a group of huge-hearted and skilled people who coordinate human organ transplant donations. After hearing the news, the event organizer and I discussed whether they would still hold the meeting and whether my topic "Living with Enthusiasm in a Transplanting World" was still appropriate. I will always be grateful to Tammy Wright for what she said to me: "Yes, we will get together for those who can make it, and yes, we will still offer your program on enthusiasm.

We need to be together and we need enthusiasm now more than ever to face the future and respond to terrorism." *This is why enthusiasm is important.*

If I needed any more confirmation, it came s week later, on September 18, when I arrived in Oklahoma City for a speaking engagement the next day. That evening I asked to visit the memorial to those whose lives were lost in the bombing there. My hosts were an inspiring high school girl, Brittany Riesenberg, and her mother, Sally, who lost friends in both Oklahoma City and New York. We talked about the future as we walked along the memorial's reflecting pool, past the 168 bronze chairs symbolizing the lives of those who were lost, and over to the lone surviving tree at the site. Brittany's enthusiasm for life and for shifting pain and anger into love and positive action through her mission work in South America again reminded me that the information in this book and others like it can be life-changing when it is acted on. *This is why enthusiasm is important.*

Vision without action is just a dream.
Action without vision just passes the time.
Vision with action can change the world.

– Loren Eiseley

After my speech the next day, a woman came up to me and said, "Your speech was great but what was most inspiring to me is that you flew here. I lost my husband in the bombing. I am scheduled to get on a plane next week and I was ready to cancel until I heard you say that even though you're afraid to fly – not just because of terrorism but also because of turbulence – you fly anyway because you feel passionate about your work. You showed me that when you remind yourself of why you do what you do, your passion allows you to overcome your fear. If you can do it, I can do it."

Did I intentionally plan that comment about passion into my speech? Not on your life. That came from enthusiasm – Spirit breathing through me – answering the need for encouragement and trust. *This is why enthusiasm is important.*

Three weeks later I flew to Albany, New York, for another speech. Between my flying jitters, speech preparation, and anticipated visit to Ground Zero, I was feeling anxious.

When I arrived at the Albany airport, my nervousness was replaced with a rush of overwhelming emotion. I couldn't stop the tears as I walked out of the terminal into the lobby along with 26 other passengers from a plane that seats 155 passengers (yes, I counted them because there were so many empty seats). We were greeted with a cheering crowd of several hundred people with children on their shoulders, babies in strollers, grandparents in wheelchairs, hailing us, waving their mini American flags, and offering smiles and hugs to everyone. Their welcome reminded me that I'd made the right decision to fly. *This is why enthusiasm is important.*

Three days later, I was at Ground Zero. Nothing could have prepared us for the reality of what we'd seen on TV. As we walked in from over a mile away, the acrid smell assaulted my nose. Part of me wanted to run home, to my safe world in San Diego. But as we reached the edges of the World Trade Center, my heart burst. For 16 square blocks, memorials of letters, photos, and memorabilia were glued, pinned, nailed, taped, and tied on every possible flat vertical surface. They paid tribute to the thousands of lost loved ones. Inside the yellow-taped police line, somber police officers and firefighters waded through debris-filled, water-slicked streets, returning smiles of welcome from the thousands of people lined up along the perimeter wanting to connect. *This is why enthusiasm is important.*

I now know deep in my soul that enthusiasm is at the heart of any positive change in the world. Each of us have something to offer to uplift the spirits of others, whether through achieving a lifelong goal that inspires children to make better choices, influencing friends to a healthier way of life, helping people heal themselves, creating a joyful workplace and home, or connecting more deeply with family, nature, or a cause. In all of its expressions, enthusiasm is a gift to be shared with the world.

Each day comes bearing its own gifts. Untie the ribbons.

– Ruth Ann Schabaker

Day 3

Accomplishing – Whistle While You Work

Would you like more energy to get more done?

a. Is this a rhetorical question?

b. Depends on how much exercise I have to do.

c. If it's fun, count me in.

d. Always. I keep a running list of 50 energy-building tips that help me get things done faster and with more fun.

~ ~ ~ ~ ~ ~ ~ ~ ~ ~ ~ ~

Accomplishing is not just about getting things done; it's also about the legacy you want to leave behind when you've moved on to that grand hotel in the sky. It's about eliminating resistance to doing what is difficult but needs to be done. It is about increasing joy while doing your tasks. It's also about reaching for your goals and dreams, including exercising, paying bills, cleaning, going back to school, getting married (or remarried), or starting a business.

Many of us are so busy procrastinating or fixating on the uncomfortable small stuff, we never get around to planning or living the good big stuff. Today we're going to focus on getting the small stuff done so when you reach Day 15 – Know What's Important – you'll have a sky full of enthusiasm to expand the big picture of your life.

Moving past your resistance to accomplishing what you consider important can be easier than you think if you put your enthusiasm to work. Enthusiasm turns "I have to" into "I want to" and "I don't want to" into "I'm doing it anyway" and "It's not fun" into "I'll make this fun." And the trick is learning how to connect your enthusiasm to whatever you want to accomplish.

Five Tips for Overcoming Procrastination and Accomplishing More

Like many people, Sandy admits that she procrastinates getting certain things done until the last minute, or not at all. In particular, she hates paying her bills, especially reconciling credit card statements. She wants to use her bank's Internet bill-paying service but hasn't had the desire to do all the detail work on the computer to set it up or download the monthly statements. "Just thinking about my bills," she sighs, "makes me comatose."

When the bills come in, she puts them in a pile on top of the corner desk in the kitchen next to the computer, the phone, and a dying plant from Aunt Gretchen. Her three children's school notes, the rest of the mail, and the morning newspaper also reside on this desk. The cat regularly visits in the morning for a little digging exercise in the plant. And after school, the children use the computer nonstop – doing homework, playing games, or instant messaging with friends until their bedtime.

Sandy promises herself, "Tonight I'll get to those bills after I put the kids to bed and finish writing my report for my committee meeting tomorrow." After she tucks in the children, she tells herself that she'll get up early to finish the report because what she really wants to do tonight is get on the Internet and research her new business idea. She and a friend want to start a mentoring program that connects "latchkey" children with "afterschool grandparents" from local Senior Center residents.

Like many women, Sandy is over-committed and undersupported. We'll talk more about support systems and asking for help (great tools for getting more done) on Day 20, but there's another element in Sandy's life that undermines her enthusiasm and ultimately her success – energy.

Sandy's energy is depleted after her kids are in bed. There's no creative juice left just for her. She tells herself, "I think I'll take a little nap." "Danger, danger," you and I call out, just like the robot cautioned the adventurous son Will in the TV show *Lost in Space* (one of my favorites as a teenager). You and I both know where this "nap" is going to lead – or at least we *think* we know. She'll sleep straight through the night without accomplishing either project.

I asked Rita Emmett, procrastination expert and author of *The Procrastinator's Handbook*, to help Sandy stop putting off her bill-paying tasks so she could direct that resistance into enthusiasm to further her business idea. Here's what Rita said:

> Sandy has a case of the dreads, which slows down or stops many people from achieving their goals. So the first thing she needs to do is acknowledge her dislike for paying bills and decide to do it anyway. The pleasure will outweigh the pain when she's finished.
>
> A second procrastination buster is to take one hour to focus only on the task at hand and push away any distractions – nothing but cleaning off the desk, paying bills, and getting the bill-paying service set up. Sandy will probably find it takes less than a half hour to do all that if she stays tightly focused. As well, her enthusiasm for getting the job done will flow over into other aspects of her life.
>
> A third tip is to determine if she's a morning or evening person. If she's a morning person, she may need to go to bed earlier and get up earlier to pay bills. If she's an evening person, she should take her nap at lunch or right after she gets home for 20 minutes, then do her creative work later in the evening. Her kids, like most others, will adjust to reasonable time limits if she is firm and consistent about setting boundaries.
>
> Fourth, she needs to create more rewards for herself. She could use her nap as a reward for keeping the bill station and desk organized. Or she could tell herself she can't use the Internet for anything else until she sets up the bill-payment service. Sandy has to act as her own wise parent.

Sandy is sitting – or rather sleeping – on a hidden goldmine that will help her realize her dream of opening her own business and her goal of managing her finances better – her nap. Yes, her nap! Used creatively, a nap easily restores energy. We'll explore the art and power of napping on Day 8 – Radiating Energy. In the meantime, don't procrastinate as you answer these two questions:

What one project or task do you put off that you'd like to do with more commitment and enthusiasm?

___

What one action will you take to move that project or task forward?

___

Make Yourself a Goal Tape to Keep Yourself on Track

My sister Eileen wanted to be a nurse from the time she was a little girl. When she reached college and discovered running, she also decided she wanted to compete in an Ironman Triathlon – a 2.5-mile swim in Hawaii's ocean, 112-mile bike ride, and 26-mile marathon completed within 17 hours – by the time she reached age 40.

Eileen became a nurse at age 22 and competed in her first Ironman Triathlon at age 35. Receiving a nursing degree is a feat in itself (God bless our nurses; I opted out of nursing school when I heard bedpans and catheters were part of the program). Getting to that first Ironman is also a huge triumph.

To qualify for the Ironman, participants must either be selected in a lottery from thousands of entrants or prequalify in a prior triathlon and come in first in their age group. Eileen trained daily with a friend for the year prior to the race and received coaching from an exercise physiologist. Because she didn't win the lottery, she competed in the prequalifying race.

During the five-hour drive to the race's starting point, she listened to the positive goal audiotape she made for herself a month earlier. In fact, she had listened to it every day to keep herself motivated. The tape included her favorite music and a script she had written and read into a tape recorder. She wrote the script in first person as if she were running the race and doing it perfectly – "I am running at my best, I overcome all obstacles, I finish first in my age group..."

When I race I'm full of doubts...who will be second, who will be third?

– Nourreddine Morceli

She did it! Eileen qualified for the Ironman! The evening after the race I called her to ask how she did and she said, "Mary, the most incredible thing happened. During that entire race, whenever I felt myself slowing down, I heard the tape in the back of my mind saying, 'You can do it. Keep going just another ten feet.' So I did and I came in first! I can't believe it! And more amazing is that generally there are about 15 to 20 seconds between each person at the finish line. But the person who finished second in my age group was 18 minutes behind me!"

Fast-forward 12 years. Eileen has accomplished these two goals and gone on to expand them. She is now a nurse practitioner at Children's Hospital in Milwaukee, Wisconsin. She is also a volunteer women's running coach for Special Olympics and an accomplished triathlete, having completed eight annual Ironman triathlons and five World Championship triathlons.

Like Eileen, you have the capacity to accomplish whatever you set out to do. Make a commitment to your goal and recommit to it on a daily basis. Not easy, but definitely worth it.

> *What I've learned in my years as a competitive wheelchair athlete is this – what separates a winner from the rest of the pack is not raw talent or physical ability; instead, it is the drive and dedication to work hard every single day, and the heart to go after your dream, no matter how unattainable others think it is.*
>
> – Linda Mastandrea

Today's Action Step

Make a list of five things you've been procrastinating about. Rate them in order of importance. Cross off #5 (this is called professionally putting off what is least important) and circle #1 (this gets you focused). Write down three things you can do to move that project or task forward. Do one before the end of the day today.

Tips for Creating More Enthusiasm

- ❑ Ask for help. Find a friend to do your task with you. (See Day 20.)
- ❑ Smile, sing, hum, or dance while you're working. It makes your body think it's happy.
- ❑ Practice the END method for any task – eliminate, negotiate, or delegate.
- ❑ Make a "positive goals" tape and listen to it in the morning and evening, and during times when you need a burst of energy.
- ❑ Make a list of ten small "accomplishment" rewards that can be done in five minutes or less. Choose from the list each time you finish *one* step of your task or goal.

Questions to Ask Yourself

- What is your most productive time of day?
- Where are your most productive places?
- What is one of your favorite daily tasks to do at home?
- What is one of your proudest accomplishments?
- What is one of your favorite ways to reward yourself?

Day 4

Influencing – May I Help You?

How easy is it for you to get other people to buy your ideas, products, or services?

a. *Let's just say that I graduated last in my class on purpose so that everyone else could get ahead.*

b. *Just call me Attila the Hun.*

c. *I'm a money magnet. If I'm excited about what I'm talking about, people throw money at me.*

d. *I finally figured out that my enthusiasm is in direct proportion to how excited I am about what I'm selling, and how much I'm helping someone who needs what I have to see the benefits in what I offer.*

~ ~ ~ ~ ~ ~ ~ ~ ~ ~ ~

A study done by the National Center on Educational Quality of the Workforce at the University of Pennsylvania found that attitude is the skill employers most look for when hiring. All things being equal, a positive attitude will get the job and especially in a sales and service culture, it keeps customers coming back for life. Customers are more willing to buy from someone they like; they continue buying from someone who is enthusiastic about the products they represent and the people they serve.

If you've ever been on a Southwest Airlines flight or shopped at a Nordstrom's department store, you know the importance they place on enthusiastic employees. These two companies breathe the message that a customer's emotional experience in their environment as well as the products they offer are key components to their success. When I fly Southwest, even though I prefer other airline's confirmed seating policy and don't like waiting in long lines, I'm always smiling by the time we take off because of the upbeat, usually humorous introduction by the flight attendant.

When I'm shopping at Nordstrom, between the pianist and the shoe department, well, does it get any better? With a size 12 foot noodging to a 13 as I grow older, the enthusiasm of Nordstrom's shoe salespeople makes me feel like Cinderella, and that is no small feat! I actually had one sales associate who not only didn't smirk or roll his eyes when I asked for a size 12M, he seemed almost giddy at the idea of being able to outfit my feet with his favorite shoe designer. When he didn't have the color I wanted, he did a quick computer check on the style, pulled out two business cards and gave me one. As he gave me one card and wrote my information on the other, he said, "I know you're traveling. We've got the color you want at another store. Let me write down your name and credit card number and we'll ship them to you free of charge and you'll pay no tax." Do you think I'm going to buy those shoes? And here's the icing on the cake: when I got to my hotel a few hours later and checked my messages at the office, there was a message from my shoe salesperson. "Ms. Marcdante, this is Scott at Nordstrom's. I just want to confirm that your size 12 medium Rangoni shoes are on their way. It was a pleasure serving you; I hope you enjoyed your stay in Seattle. We enjoyed having you here."

Besides Scott's personal work ethic, what helps him work with such enthusiasm? Maybe it's the Nordstrom philosophy. Their employee handbook is a five-by-eight-inch gray card that reads:

> We're glad to have you with our company. Our number one goal is to provide outstanding customer service. Set both your personal and professional goals high. We have great confidence in your ability to achieve them. Rule #1: Use your good judgment in all situations. There will be no additional rules. Please feel free to ask your department manager, store manager, or division general manager any question at any time.

Enthusiasm is written all over Nordstrom's seven-sentence policy with words like "glad," "number one goal," "outstanding customer service," "set your goals high," and "great confidence in your ability to achieve."

What words of enthusiasm are you using to describe your business, service, product, or idea to others? List three in the spaces below..

_______________ _______________ _______________

We Buy Perceived Enthusiasm

Roxanne Emmerich, author of *Thank God, It's Monday: How to Build a Motivating Workplace,* explains enthusiasm at work in this way:

> Influencing anyone in business really comes down to this: Businesses work better when people sell things. In fact, it's necessary. People always think that they can sell things by telling about it, but the reality is that we all buy for emotional reasons. We buy perceived enthusiasm from the person delivering the message. People who believe that they sell are never great at selling. People who can't hardly stand themselves unless they're getting up in the morning and perceiving their job to be helping people – in other words, selling things – tend not to be able to do anything but sell.

All It Takes Is 30 Seconds

Beth, a manager of a large warehouse store, says, "We have over 10 checkout lanes in our store, each with a different personality behind the register. On busy days, the lines can reach five to ten people long at certain times. I noticed that even when we open up a new checkout lane, the lines managed by certain checkers always remain longer. Customers will stand in line an extra five minutes just to hear that clerk say, 'Good morning, Mr. Smith. You're going to love that salmon. And it's such a great price this week! Good choice!' All it takes is 30 seconds and a few acknowledging sentences said with an enthusiastic tone to create customer loyalty."

It's Important That You Get Exactly What You Want

Maybe you've heard the common hiring statement, "Hire for attitude, train for skill." Granted, being skilled at your job is important. But sometimes attitude is even more important. Especially when things don't go as planned.

I recently moved into a new apartment community. For one month prior to my move, I had explored the new development complex at various times of the day to make sure I was choosing a quiet location. I needed peace and quiet during my writing sabbaticals. I was so excited to find a unit that had a beautiful canyon view with morning sunrises and the mountains of Mexico off in the far distance.

The movers were 20 minutes into their scheduled two-hour move-in when the deafening sound of fighter jets roared through the canyon. We all stood outside at attention, stunned by the close range of military aircraft in the sky. When another jet appeared and then another, nonstop for over ten minutes, my mind raced. "Hold the move!" I yelled above the sound. "I've got to check this out. We may be going into storage." (On top of all this, I was leaving the next day for a seven-day business trip.) As I ran to the leasing office in a panic, my mind flashing on the ten-page lease agreement that had a one-sentence clause I overlooked in my desire for the canyon view – "Aircraft Overflights."

When I reached the office, Jennifer, my leasing consultant, greeted me with a smile. She quickly noticed my concern, jumped out of her chair, asked what was wrong and how she could help. I explained the situation, to which she replied, "Let's go check it out together. I want you to be really happy here and if it's not right, remember you have 30 days to make a decision. Would you like to look at another unit on the other side of the property?" When we got to the unit, the jet noise was still so loud we could barely hear each other. She agreed that it would be impossible for me to write in these circumstances. She also said, "In all the times I've been out on the grounds, I've never heard the jets so loud that it would interfere with conversation. Maybe there are special circumstances causing this. But regardless, if it's not right for you, we'll do everything we can to help you find something that is, even if it means helping you find a quieter community." She smiled her Crest-toothpaste smile and I told the movers to continue. In less than three minutes, she had relieved my concern and, without effort, persuaded me to stay at least through the trial period. That's the power of enthusiasm – the ability to show someone such a strong level of passion, interest, and concern for a person, situation, and product that even in difficult situations, people give you the benefit of the doubt, do business with you again, and refer you to their friends.

> *When work, commitment, and pleasure all become one and you reach that deep well where passion lives, nothing is impossible.*
>
> – Nancy Coey

It's now six months later and I love where I live. Jennifer and her Torrey Ridge colleagues have not only kept me happy but also this entire community. The Irvine Apartment Communities, the parent company for our community, recently awarded the Torrey Ridge Team their company's Superior Customer Service Award for being one of the top three complexes out of 70, based on resident satisfaction. And the rest of the story? My jets tell me like clockwork when it's time to get my workday started – 7:30 in the morning. Depending on their monthly training patterns, throughout the day they remind me to stop what I'm doing, take a deep breath, and give thanks that what is in the air, as a Marine helicopter mechanic said to me, is "The sound of peace."

There Is a Way to Ask "How Are You!?"

I wish I could bottle Jennifer's enthusiasm and give it away. Since I can't, I decided the best way I could help you benefit from Jennifer's success was to interview her. As you read her answer, think about how you would answer. And feel free to use this question with people you find enthusiastic. The more you explore, question, and apply these ideas, the better you will become at influencing others.

I asked Jennifer, "How has your enthusiasm helped you become successful?" Jennifer is one of the top leasing agents month after month in a company with over 130 leasing agents in southern California. Here's what she said:

> People come to me when they need a place to live. It could be a happy or devastating event. It could be a marriage, a divorce, or even a death in the family. It's important for me to know and understand why someone

> is moving. It's not about the sale; it's about a true desire to fix their current situation. I ask a ton of open-ended questions and I listen to what they're saying. Many people think sales is about the "gift of gab," but I believe it's really about actively listening to what people have to say. There is a way to ask "How are you?" and there is a way to ask "How are you!?" My interest in them is not for my job; it's just who I am.
>
> People know when you are truly listening to them versus when you are going through the motions. They can sense enthusiasm and they feed off of it. If I didn't show enthusiasm with customers, they wouldn't feel enthusiastic about living in my community. To me, it's a pretty simple equation.

Jennifer's enthusiastic attitude is expressed by her welcoming smile, her eye contact, the positive energy in her voice, the questions she asks, and her interest in the details of the other person's life. Her attention is very focused and upbeat. It's a successful combination that wins customers and friends and keeps them for life. Enthusiasm works!

> *I consider my ability to arouse enthusiasm among men the greatest asset I possess. The way to develop the best that is in a man is by appreciation and encouragement.*
>
> – Charles Schwab

Today's Action Step

Look for someone who has a need you can fill and give it your enthusiastic best. If your child asks you for a snack, your spouse wants to know where the keys to the car are, or a coworker wants to know where a file is, act as if you work for Southwest Airlines or Nordstrom's and turn on the charm to help them. If no one's asked for your help by noon, ask someone what you can do to make his or her life easier in the next hour. I guarantee it will shock some people and delight others.

Tips for Creating More Enthusiasm

- ❑ Give more than you expect to get. Under-promising and over-delivering still work.
- ❑ Paint pictures of pleasurable experiences when you speak to others. Treat all people as if they're extremely important. Smile, offer a handshake, and hold your smile while you look into their eyes for a second longer than they look at you.
- ❑ Ask people how they are, *and listen*, before you offer your thoughts, problems, or advice.
- ❑ Before you call someone, put a smile on your face. People can "hear" a smile.
- ❑ Decide to make people around you smile. Be witty. Memorize a favorite funny line and use it to diffuse tension with others.

Questions to Ask Yourself

- What aspects of your work are you passionate about?
- Describe a time when you persuaded someone to see your point of view and it led to a better way of doing things. What were the key things you did to make that happen?
- What is one of the best customer service experiences you've had? What did they do? How can you apply that to your life?
- What is one thing you could do to add more enthusiasm to your workday?
- What is one thing you could stop doing or change that would give you more enthusiasm for your work?

Day 5

Healing – The Doctor Is In

How would you rate your health over the last 12 months?

a. Between my Prozac, Mylanta, and Advil, I'm doing great.

b. One or two colds, a few headaches, and several pains in the neck, depending on the mood of my boss, co-worker, or child.

c. Since I've had cancer, my whole definition of healthy has changed. How am I? Alive, smiling, and grateful – that's healthy to me.

d. Since I started eating smaller portions with more green veggies, doing some kind of exercise every day, and upping my fun factor, I'm healthier than ever.

~ ~ ~ ~ ~ ~ ~ ~ ~ ~ ~ ~

Health is wealth. I remember when my father was going through chemotherapy for lymphatic cancer. He was 62 and I had just turned 26. He said to me, "You're healthy now. Take care of yourself. Do a better job than I did. You just don't know how important health is until you lose it. When you have your health, you have everything you need."

> *Maybe we each need to pay our doctors to sit us down and look us in the eye and say, "You are going to die. Get it?" Because those words apply to every one of us. The only part we don't know is when. What a difference it makes, not knowing when.*
>
> – C. Leslie Charles

Dad went on to live another 15 years, which honestly surprised me. (And he didn't die from cancer, but from a bacterial infection he contracted following knee replacement surgery.) He was overweight by at least 75 pounds, drank too much, smoked, and had a temper that made me run when I was a teenager. But as I learned more about the healing power of enthusiasm, I realized he likely survived as long as he did because he was determined not to let life take the best of him. Despite his lack of self-care, my father lived "big" – people knew when he walked into a room. When he laughed, he roared and easily drew others in on the fun.

The more enthusiasm you have, the healthier you feel and the faster you heal, whether you're recovering from an illness, accident, broken heart, death of a loved one, end of a marriage, or any other type of loss. Research has now proven that laughter, optimism, and a will to live – all aspects of enthusiasm – speed up healing time and increase well-being and longevity. Dr. Norman Cousins discovered in the 1970s that laughter and a positive attitude could heal disease. He healed himself after doctors had given up on him. Scientists have developed a new field of medicine called psychoneuroimmunology – the connection between our mind, emotions, nervous system, and independent immune systems.

Each of these systems contributes to or is affected by enthusiasm – that flow of joyful energy through us. Because it's such a broad topic, today we'll focus on enthusiasm and healing from the perspective of an optimistic attitude, which is one of the core characteristics of enthusiastic people (you'll learn about the key characteristics in Chapter 3).

Optimism and Healing

The conclusions of two studies worth noting for their direct association to various aspects of optimism and physical healing include:

- *Optimistic people have fewer problems after heart surgery.* With heart disease being the leading killer of women and the fact that more women die during their first heart attack than men, this is a powerful study to take seriously. Carnegie Mellon University measured the effects of optimism on a group of heart bypass patients – 70 percent men, 30 percent women with an average age of 62. The results showed that the optimistic patients were 50 percent less like likely to have follow-up problems (including everything from wound infection to heart attack and additional angioplasty) and 77 percent were less likely to be hospitalized in the following six months.

- *Optimistic women have less stress during pregnancy and give birth to healthier babies.* Whether you're a pregnant woman or know of one, this information can make birthing easier. Marci Lobel, Ph.D., and her colleagues at the Department of Psychology, State University of New York at Stony Brook determined that optimistic women, compared with pessimistic women, delivered healthier babies closer to full term and experienced less prenatal stress. Ratings for optimism were based on future expectations, coping skills, and perceived control over the birth. One of the most interesting pieces of data is that optimistic women were less likely to use avoidance behavior (not thinking about the birth, sleeping more, avoiding people). This gave them a stronger sense of control and an easier pregnancy.

Optimism Can Be Learned

Whether you're pregnant with your first or fourth child, coping with heart disease, recovering from a cold or flu, or simply wanting to live a longer, healthier life, optimism is worth cultivating. And according to Martin Seligman, Ph.D., author of *Learned Optimism* and *Authentic Happiness*, optimism *can* be learned. Optimism can also help you partner successfully with your health care professionals.

Find an Optimistic Physician to Help You Heal

Six years ago, following my annual pap smear, I received a call from my gynecologist's office saying the doctor wanted to see me regarding the results. I told the nurse I was going out of town later in the day and would be gone for a week. She replied, "Then he can see you in an hour." I hung up the phone, called my sister Jeanne, and when I heard her voice, I burst into tears. "I'm going to die. I know it," I cried. Ah yes, I, the stress management expert, lost it, but for good reason. Ever since my father's lymphoma diagnosis and my mother's death from ovarian cancer six years earlier, I had worried about my fibroids and benign ovarian cysts. But I never expected to get "the call." I was an optimist and optimists don't get cancer! At least not *this* optimist.

> *Am I like the optimist who, while falling ten stories from a building, says at each story, "I'm all right so far"?*
>
> – Gretel Ehrlich

"Please, have a seat. I have good news and bad news," my doctor said. "The good news is you don't have cancer. The bad news is: yet. You have a type of cancer cell that hasn't invaded the cervical tissues yet. We recommend a hysterectomy because the cells jump around like fleas and if we don't get them all, within six months to two years, you'll be back in here with full blown cancer, a radical hysterectomy with lymph node removal and radiation. Take a few days to think about it and explore your options. I know you prefer alternative therapies, so we'll support you in whatever way we can."

Three days later, I arranged to have surgery. After explaining the procedure, my doctor asked if there was anything special I needed or wanted to ensure that I felt safe and comfortable during my surgery and hospital stay. Having talked with other women and done Internet research, I said, "Yes, two things." Here they are:

> No negative humor while I'm being operated on. Only positive statements from you and your team, like, "Mary, you're doing great! Everything's going super."
>
> I would like to use some audiotapes that have been proven to lessen anxiety, reduce the amount of anesthesia needed and speed up recovery time. There's an operating room tape to keep me asleep and relaxed, and there's a post-op tape that wakes me up and reduces pain. The only

challenge is that I'll need someone to change the tapes on my Walkman while I'm under.

He smiled and said, "I haven't had those kinds of requests before but I think we can handle them. I'll take care of the first one and if the anesthesiologist or your operating room nurse agrees to the second one, you'll be all set."

Three weeks later I was in the pre-op room, being prepared for surgery. The anesthesiologist paid a visit and, with a big smile, said, "I hear you have an extra job for me today, to change a few audiotapes and watch your breathing." I reminded him, "Just to be sure, breathing is first priority, and tapes are second." He chuckled and said he'd see me in surgery.

I was alone in this giant freezer of a room, trying to be upbeat to keep myself in the "right" healing frame of mind, yet I was scared to death. I'd only been in a hospital to visit sick people, not to be one. I took a deep breath. My mind started wandering. Interestingly, what kicked in were my words on the first tape I had been listening to every night while I slept for the past three weeks: "Counting down, 20, 19, 18, you're relaxing, 17, 16, 15, breathe through your fear, 14, 13..." Suddenly I was jarred out of my reverie. The doors to the operating room opened. I felt like I was on the set of the television series *ER*.

My quiet, usually reserved physician came charging through the double doors surrounded by a team of nurses and an assistant surgeon. In a booming voice he said, "Mary Marcdante, you're going to do great. Everything's going to turn out super!" He turned to his staff and, with the energy of a football coach leading his team to victory, he yelled out, "Is Mary Marcdante going to heal quickly? Are we going to do a great job for her?" They all cheered a loud "Yes!" and began applauding.

Can you imagine? He used my *exact* words and his enthusiasm included everyone around us. I don't know who was laughing harder as they wheeled me into the operating room, them or me. And the smiles lasted until my eyes closed shut on the operating table.

Maybe you've been in a similar situation: You fall into that emotional place where you meet the scared child within who says, "You know, you could die. They could open you up and they could find a whole lot of cancer in there. This isn't fun. I want my mom!" You wonder if you'll ever find your way out. And then if someone comes along in the midst of that dark night (or day) of the soul and offers you hope, suddenly you are renewed. You're back swimming in an ocean of enthusiasm.

I'll never be able to prove that my optimistic attitude or that of my physician saved my life, but I believe it helped. I'm here today, healthy, and cancer-free, in large part because of an enthusiastic surgeon and team of nurses who willingly expanded their vision of medicine to include the healing of my body, mind, *and* spirit.

> *Enthusiasm, like measles, mumps and the common cold, is highly contagious.*
>
> – Emory Ward

Today's Action Step

Set up appointments for your annual physical, mammogram, pap smear, bone density test, cholesterol test, and a colonoscopy (if you're over 50 or have a history of colon cancer in your family).

Tips for Creating More Enthusiasm

- ❑ Schedule a massage or spa with your best friend in the next 30 days.
- ❑ Buy yourself a CD of healing music and listen to it once a day for the next week.
- ❑ Take on a healing adventure by trying something you've never imagined yourself doing – painting, acting, rock climbing.
- ❑ Send your doctor's office flowers or a box of candy (it keeps them enthusiastic!).
- ❑ Thank your body every day for all that it does to keep you healthy.

Questions to Ask Yourself

- How would you describe your parents' attitudes toward health?
- How have your parents' health or attitudes about health affected your own attitude?
- Do you need to change any of your beliefs to become healthier?
- What does your body need that you're willing to do to keep it healthier?
- What has your experience been with your health providers' attitudes toward your health? Is there anything you could do to strengthen relationships with your doctor and staff and encourage them to be more optimistic?

Day 6

Enjoying – Don't Worry, Be Happy

Do you have enough *fun* and *joy* in your life?

a. *Please, send in the clowns…*

b. *I want to put the "fun" back in "dysfunctional."*

c. *I am the life of my party. And life is the party I make.*

d. *I do. I'm reading a great book –* Living with Enthusiasm *– that shows me when I combine fun with meaning and contribution, the result is joy.*

~ ~ ~ ~ ~ ~ ~ ~ ~ ~ ~

Leslie rides horses for enjoyment. Dianne plays her cello and Sue works at the office after everyone's gone home, catching up on projects while listening to her favorite classical music. Kym curls up with a good book, or takes a long hot shower sitting in the bathtub. After trying to read in the shower, she discovered doing both at once does not double her pleasure.

Each of us may define and experience enjoyment in different ways but we share one common desire – we all want more enjoyment in our lives. It doesn't take a million-dollar research study to answer the question, "Would you like to enjoy your life more?" However, because some people enjoy conducting surveys, polls, and research studies, we have many resources from which to draw that prove we are a pleasure-seeking, pain-avoiding species. The more joy we can squeeze out of life, the happier we are.

This is where enthusiasm comes in. I love the saying, "Half of life is learning how to get what you want and the other half is learning how to enjoy what you get." How much more could you enjoy yourself if you had more enthusiasm? In her well-researched book, *The Pleasure Zone,* psychologist Stella Resnick says, "What does make a difference [in how happy a person is] relates much more to a person's level of enthusiasm, energy and their willingness to derive pleasure from ordinary life."

How Happy Are You?

Let's look at your overall level of happiness. Are you happy most of the time? Some of the time? Or do you live in neutral? In a happiness survey developed by Michael W. Fordyce and reported in *Authentic Happiness* by Martin Seligman, Ph.D., 3,050 American adults were asked how happy they were. The average score (out of 10) was 6.92. Their findings reported that 54 percent of people say they are happy, 20 percent say they are unhappy, and 26 percent are neutral. What percentage of the time would you say you feel...

Happy _______% Unhappy _______% Neutral_______%

Would you like to raise your "happy" percentage by one or two percentage points or perhaps even reach double digits? That's definitely our goal for *Living with Enthusiasm*. Use the tips and techniques in the **21-Day Smile Diet** to help you consciously choose to increase your happiness by a few points every day. Think of enthusiasm like a bank account that earns interest. Every time you consciously choose to do anything with a little more enthusiasm, you're earning interest that is deposited in your enthusiasm account. That way, when you encounter difficult times, you can draw on the interest that accumulates over time.

What Do You Enjoy Doing?

Today is about discovering what makes you smile, what brings you joy, and *enjoying* it. To help you warm up your joy muscles, write down your favorite...

Activity ____

Hobby/Sport ____

Art/Music ____

Flower ____

Food ____

Scent ____

Place in nature _____________________________________

Other ____

How did it feel to think about things that make you happy? Did you savor the experience or motor through it? Did you skip over these questions because you didn't want to take the time? Don't feel guilty if you skipped this exercise; just notice it may indicate other places in your life where you deny or limit the ways in which you enjoy yourself.

Go back to your list and circle the one that gives you the most pleasure. Sit back in your chair (or wherever you're reading), put a smile on your face, take two or three long deep breaths, and imagine experiencing your favorite activity or place in nature (or whatever you circled). Commit to actually have that experience in real time within the next week.

Joy is the feeling of grinning on the inside.
– Dr. Melba Colgrove

What Is Your Bliss Quota?

My first memories of enjoying myself are filled with images of kindergarten show 'n tells and sing-alongs, overnights at my grandparent's house snuggled up with "Gramma" in front of their new television eating popcorn and watching *The Ed Sullivan Show*, fishing at the turtle pond with my father in an old aluminum rowboat, playing grown-up in my mother's clothes, and rescuing every stray cat, dog, mole, and orphan bird that fell out of its nest.

As I grew older, I became more serious and anxious. My mother's clinical depression became the focal point around which my life revolved. Making my mother's tears and headaches turn into smiles and laughter became a measuring stick for my happiness. It was only through working with several great therapists over the years that I discovered how I censored joy. It's not that joy wasn't in my life – it's that I didn't know how to let it in. If grades were given for how well one mastered "Depression 101," I would have received an A+.

While in my late 30s, I remember one counseling session in which the therapist said, "What brings you pleasure?"

"Making others happy," I cheerily replied.

"And what do you do when they're not happy?"

"I try to cheer them up."

"And what if it doesn't work?"

"I try harder," I said, my voice starting to quiver.

"And what if they're angry with you or don't like something you've done?"

"I feel anxious and try to appease them."

"What if that doesn't work, how do you feel?"

"Not very good," I hesitantly offered, almost in tears.

"So what will you do to make yourself feel better?"

"I don't know," I whispered.

My therapist then said, "So here is your task: Spend the next week noticing what makes *you* feel good that has nothing to do with other people. You're already skilled at that. And when you notice that good feeling, also notice how long it lasts. If it's a minute, see if you can hold it for two." She handed me a poem as I was leaving and said, "Think about this. You're not alone."

I thought, "I have my homework cut out for me." This memory makes me smile now because, even then, looking for joy was "work." I took my favorite drive along the lake and noticed my first moment of joy as I drove past "Duck Lagoon." That's where Dad took us kids on weekends and where we fed the ducks. I felt a buttery warmth melt over me and a smile spread across my face. "Oh, here it is. Joy. Yippee! Darn, I forgot to call my client back." Boom. In less than just a few *seconds,* the joy was gone. One thought and it was over. Fifteen minutes later, I was almost in tears again realizing how easily I shifted from joy to what was "wrong" or what I needed to "fix."

BLISS QUOTA
What is your Bliss Quota?
An hour per day?
Or an hour per month?
What are the limits of your joy?

Find out how long you can feel
Exquisitely contented.
Consciously allow that time to increase.

Be aware of how uncomfortable it is
To experience more Happiness than usual.

This awareness alone,
Without doing anything else,
Will allow more Love
Into Your Life.

– Peter Rengel

Sound familiar? What if we stopped thinking we had to "fix" ourselves or the rest of the planet? What if we decided that who we are is just perfect right now, that we could enjoy all the beauty that is in front of us, behind us, around us, and inside us? I believe that rekindling joy and wonder in adults is the answer to inner peace *and* maybe even world peace. I know, I know, this sounds like a TV commercial sound-bite solution to a huge problem, but let that thought sit for a bit. Notice how often you live in a war zone between joy and fear, joy and anger, joy and self-doubt, joy and guilt, or joy and despair. Who wins? Yes, duality is part of the human condition; without fear, anger, self-doubt, guilt, or despair, we could not know joy. But what if we decided to share more of our joy instead of our problems and irritations? What if we encouraged each other to enjoy each other's successes instead of seeing them as threats to our self-esteem? What if we spent the first 15 minutes of any meeting, school class, or family meal asking at least one of these questions: "What's great with your life today? What made you smile today? What brought you the most joy yesterday? Who did you share your joy with today?"

Think of all the beauty still left around you and be happy.
– Anne Frank

Today's Action Step

Choose one activity you love doing and one activity you have to do but dislike doing. Consciously choose to do the activity you love doing with a little more awareness of how much you love doing it. When you're doing the activity you dislike, put a smile on your face and decide you're going to find some way to make it fun.

Tips for Enjoying

- ❑ Keep a Joy Journal. Record joyful moments. Aim for one a day. Three to five a day gets you extra credit.
- ❑ Call a friend and talk with each other about what brought you joy as children, and the ways your parents expressed their enjoyment.
- ❑ Make a list of 100 (okay, start with 25) places, things, ideas that you think you might enjoy doing before the end of your life.
- ❑ When you notice you're feeling good, smile. It tells your body and your mind you're enjoying yourself.
- ❑ Who are some of the most joy-filled people you know? What is one behavior they exhibit or activity they do that you could incorporate into your life to feel more joy?

Questions to Ask Yourself

- What are you most looking forward to in the next 30 days?
- Who do you know who really enjoys his/her life? What is one thing that person does that you can do to help you enjoy yourself more?
- What three things do you do to pamper yourself? When will you do them next?
- What will you do for yourself in the next 24 hours to increase your bliss quota?
- What is the most outrageously enjoyable experience you could imagine giving yourself? What one step can you take today to bring that experience closer to you?

Day 7

Loving – All You Need Is Love

How connected do you feel to the people in your life?

a. *Like, totally! I love my cell phone.*

b. *Does the Internet count?*

c. *My family drives me crazy but I wouldn't trade them for a million dollars . . . at least this week. Just kidding. I love them to death and they'll be the death of me. Did I just say that?*

d. *My mother taught me that if I smile and do something every day that would cause a family member, friend, coworker, or even a stranger to say thank you, I'd never feel alone. She was right.*

~ ~ ~ ~ ~ ~ ~ ~ ~ ~

Simple as it sounds, most people prefer to be friends with, or fall in love with, an upbeat, enthusiastic person. If you've ever been around a confirmed critic or sad sack, you know that over time, when you see this person coming, you want to run the other way. If they call on the phone, as soon as you hear their voice, you find some excuse to hang up and say you will call them later. Later, you conveniently forget to return the call. It's quite the opposite when an enthusiastic friend calls to share her good news, a smiling coworker stops by your office to report that your project just got approved, or an appreciative spouse brings home your favorite flowers.

There are so many ways to share your enthusiasm with others, and few are more powerful than with those we hold most dear. Your ability to express the different facets of enthusiasm in your relationships (from appreciation to optimism to curiosity about their interests) deepens your connection, lets you resolve differences more easily, and helps the people in your life feel better about themselves.

> *We do not believe in ourselves until someone reveals that deep inside us is valuable, worth listening to, worthy of our trust, sacred to our touch. Once we believe in ourselves we can risk curiosity, wonder, spontaneous delight or any experience that reveals the human spirit.*
>
> – e.e. cummings

Even Babies Recognize Enthusiasm

Psychologist Jeffrey Cohn, Ph.D., of the University of Pittsburgh did a study with healthy mothers and their infants. He asked the mothers to smile and then show a depressed face. Immediately the infants attempted to change their mother's frown with smiles, gurgling, and reaching out. While the experiment only lasted three minutes, each of the babies immediately withdrew physically from their sad-faced mother long before the allotted time was up. Even more surprising was that when the mothers resumed their normal behavior, the babies continued to be withdrawn for up to a minute afterwards.

Babies aren't the only ones who attempt to turn a sad face into a happy one. In a study reported in *Psychology Today,* men and women were asked what they have done most often to make someone smile. The survey shows:

- Women smile themselves (28 percent) or hug (18 percent).
- Men tell a funny story (24 percent).
- Men are more likely than women to say they want to see more smiles from their spouses.
- When it comes to getting a child to smile, women (33 percent) hug and men (32 percent) act silly.

Create an Encouragement Tape for Family Members

When my nephew Tom was 11 months old, doctors discovered a cyst on his brain during his well-baby check. The week before his first birthday, they operated to relieve the pressure. The night before his surgery, I joined my brother, his wife, and their best friends to prepare Tom for his hospital stay. We sat on the living room carpet in a circle with Tom in the middle and turned on a tape recorder for an hour before Tom's bedtime. We sang him songs and told him over and over that he was a strong boy and he would get through the surgery easily and grow up to be a bright, healthy person who would make a big contribution to the world. We tickled, hugged, and kissed him into fits of laughter, and read him his favorite stories, all of which was captured on the audiotape. During his two-week hospital stay, his mother played the tape during his naps and at night to soothe and calm him. Tom is now a healthy, enthusiastic 15-year-old budding artist, who enjoys Boy Scouts and the prospect of getting his driver's license. Enthusiasm connects families and heals lives.

> *If you have only one smile in you, give it to the people you love. Don't be surly at home, then go out in the street and start grinning "Good morning" at total strangers.*
>
> – Maya Angelou

Give Them Five-to-One

The University of Washington and the Seattle Marital and Family Institute discovered powerful data that shows the importance of enthusiasm in marriage. In his fascinating book *The Seven Principles for Making Marriage Work*, John Gottman, Ph.D., a cofounder of the Institute and professor at the university, reports that he can predict with 91 percent accuracy which of the 650 marriages studied would succeed or fail. "I can make this prediction," he writes, "after listening to the couple interact in our Love Lab for as little as five minutes!" He discovered that one of the common denominators in successful marriages is positive feedback – specifically a minimum of five positive comments, actions, or gestures for every one negative expressed. As you'll discover in Day 10, "focusing on the good" is a key trait of enthusiastic people and the "five-to-one" factor a good one to practice in any close relationship.

Twas the Night b4 Christmas

Sometimes our enthusiasm is expressed in the sounds of our voices. Other times, it's in the way we ask questions or in the gifts of love we offer to another.

One year about two weeks before Christmas, my father called wanting to know what was on my wish list. I mentioned a particular book and then interrupted myself and said excitedly, "Wait! What I'd really like is for you to put *The Night Before Christmas* story on audiotape."

There was this long pause. Then Dad said with a familiar sternness in his voice, "Oh for God's sake, Mary. What in the Sam Hill do you want that for? You're 40 years old!" I paused, feeling embarrassed. But I was also determined. "Dad, I remember how good it felt when we were little and cuddled up next to you while you read *The Night Before Christmas*. I can still remember how strong your voice was, how safe I felt, and how well you acted out all the different sounds and voices. I'd really appreciate your doing this. Since I'm 2500 miles away and not coming home for Christmas, it would be great to have you with me."

Dad said, with a little more softness and some incredulity, "You mean you want me to read just like I did when you were kids, with all the bells and whistles and everything?"

"Yesssssss! Just like that!" I said enthusiastically.

Again, he paused for a long time. Then he said, "I'll buy you the book."

I heard the finality of his decision in his voice and resignedly said, "Okay. Talk to you on Christmas." We said our "I love you's" and hung up. I was disappointed but tried to understand. I assumed I was asking for too much sentimentalism from a 76-year-old bear, and that, in his mind, this was a foolish request for a grown daughter to ask. Maybe. Maybe not. All I knew was that each time I talked to Dad, his voice sounded more and more tired, and I was beginning to accept that the question was no longer if, but when, the day would come that I wouldn't hear his laugh anymore.

On Christmas Eve day, a small, brown, recycled padded envelope with lots of staples and tape arrived. My name and address were written in architect's lettering with thick black magic marker, my dad's unmistakable hand. Inside was an audiotape with a handwritten label, "Twas the Night b4 Christmas."

I popped the tape in the recorder and my father's words roared, "Twas the niiiiiiiiiiiiiight before Christmas when allllllllllllllllll through the houwwwwwwwwwwwwwse," just like when we were children! When he finished, he went on to say, "And now I'm going to read from *The Little Engine That Could*." I guess Dad had another message in mind when he included a favorite childhood bedtime story he had read over and over to us when we were small. It was the same story we read to Mom when she was living with cancer three years earlier.

The tape continued with the Mormon Tabernacle Choir singing, "Silent Night," our family's favorite Christmas Eve sing-along song. And then, "Oh Come All Ye Faithful"...with more favorite songs until the tape ran out.

I went to sleep feeling safe and sound that Christmas Eve, thanking God for giving me another Christmas miracle with my dad.

The following May, Dad passed away unexpectedly. No more phone calls every Sunday morning asking me, "What was the Gospel about today, Mary?" No more "I love you's." But his voice lives on...and continues to remind me that I can do what I put my mind to; that I can stretch emotionally for someone else, even when it's difficult. That's the power of love.

I saved the tape as a surprise for my sisters and brother and their families for Christmas the following year. My youngest sister called and left a tearful message on my voice mail that said, "Mary, I just got the tape. Did you know that on the tape he said it was December 19? That's today! While I was in the living room and put on the tape, Holden (her two-and-a-half-year-old son) came running out from the kitchen full steam, yelling at the top of his lungs, 'Mommy, Grampa's here! Grampa's here!' You should have seen him, Mary, looking all around for Dad. Dad *was* here."

The sounds of enthusiasm and love live on.

Today's Action Step

Choose a family member or friend with whom to practice the "five-to-one" ratio: before the end of the day give that person five hugs, positive comments, conscious smiles, or a note of appreciation. Even offer to do a chore, run an errand, or cook their favorite meal to show your enthusiasm.

Tips for Creating More Enthusiasm

- ❑ Record an audiotape of your favorite songs and children's books and give copies to people in your family as a gift.
- ❑ Commit to five hugs a day. If there's no one around, hug yourself. It's good for your immune system.
- ❑ Call some elderly relatives and re-establish a heart connection. Share fond memories and ask them to share some of their own.
- ❑ Make friends with a young mother and share smiles with her baby. It keeps your enthusiasm muscles in good shape.
- ❑ Call one of your friends when you know he or she isn't home. When you leave a message, say, "Hello fabulous (name). This is one of your many fans. I'm so glad you're in my life. I love you."

Questions to Ask Yourself

- How often do you share your enthusiasm with the people in your family?
- How is enthusiasm for each other expressed in your family?
- What has been one of your favorite expressions of love from another person?
- Who needs the "five-to-one" from you?
- What loving gesture could you ask a family member or friend to do for you that would make them feel good for doing it?

Chapter Three

What Are the Characteristics of Enthusiastic People?

It's the fire in my eyes
And the flash of my teeth
The swing of my waist
And the joy in my feet.
– Maya Angelou

You're nine days into the **21-Day Smile Diet** and about to embark on a week of exploring the six characteristics of enthusiastic people. Before you move forward, let's celebrate how far you've come.

- ✓ You've learned about the power of your smile and the science behind it.
- ✓ You've energized yourself by waking up with the 16-second smile ritual and the five-minute smile and gratitude meditation.
- ✓ You've learned about the science of enthusiasm and that enthusiasm can be measured in the areas of work, healing, relationships, life enjoyment, and personal accomplishment.
- ✓ You've improved your performance and ability to get things done using enthusiasm as a procrastination buster.
- ✓ You've developed new ways of using enthusiasm to communicate better with others at work.

- ✓ You've discovered the power of optimism (a key trait of enthusiastic people – and one that keeps your body healthy).
- ✓ And you now have 25 new tips and techniques to increase your enjoyment, enrich your friendships, and deepen the love in your life.

How is it going so far? Have you noticed that you're smiling more often? Have you raised your bliss quota or are you stuck somewhere? Have you shared any of the daily tips with anyone else? What changes have you noticed? Write your observations below.

____

____

What's been most helpful so far?

____

What single action have you taken that has helped you live with more enthusiasm these past seven days?

____

What Does Enthusiasm Look Like?

If you ever want to see enthusiasm at its most charismatic, watch TV infomercials. You know what I'm talking about if you've written down an 800 number or reached for the phone, ready to buy, yet had no need for the product being sold. Church services are also a great place to experience enthusiasm. A good spiritual leader can rouse even the most staid and stingy to contribute their time and money to their mission. And when children are excited about anything, they provide wonderful examples of enthusiasm.

> *Whether they burst with excitement or simmer quietly, when you're in the presence of enthusiastic people, you feel happier and more excited about your life, perhaps you even feel inspired...*
>
> – Mary Marcdante

We're drawn in by the energy and passion that enthusiastic people have for their idea, product, or desire. Their voice, body language (smiling, direct eye contact, open body posture), and deep conviction mesmerize us into following them, just as children followed the mythical Pied Piper. Enthusiastic people are energy-givers. Enthusiastic people inspire us to become more confident, open, and alive; they help us be our best and share ourselves more willingly with others.

Highly enthusiastic people possess six characteristics (listed below), which we're addressing, one a day for the next six days. I'm using famous people as examples to help you quickly identify these traits. You'll see that each person has a unique way of expressing enthusiasm. While all of these individuals express their own brand of enthusiasm, not all of them exhibit all six characteristics. Yet an energetic component is common to every one. Though their enthusiasm is hard to describe, you recognize the energy and feel it when you're in their presence.

As you read through the definitions and names that follow, think of people in your own life who match these characteristics. If you don't recognize all of those listed, I hope you'll be curious and do an online search at www.google.com to learn about them. Also think about yourself and where your strengths are. Take the quiz following the descriptions to help you determine what to pay extra attention to over the next six days. The more you can connect the information you find to your everyday life and relationships, the more enthusiasm will flow through you and the richer your experiences will be.

Characteristics of Enthusiastic People

DAY 8: They **radiate energy**. They have a spring in their steps, a genuine smile, and bright eyes. When they walk into a room, heads turn and people gather. Also referred to as charisma, their power comes from within. Examples: Mother Teresa, Tina Turner, Julia Roberts, Katie Couric, Bill Clinton, Maya Angelou, my fabulous nephews, and the children you love.

DAY 9: They are **curious and interested in life**. They ask many questions and explore what interests them. They love learning and live in a state of wonder, surprise, and delight. Examples: Anna Quindlen, Sylvia Earl,

Jacques Cousteau, Maya Angelou, Marie Curie, the Delaney Sisters, any four year old.

DAY 10: They **focus on the good** (even when things are bad) and emphasize what they *can* do rather than what they *can't* do. They look for the gift in difficulties and live with gratitude. Examples: Anne Frank, Jackie Pflug, Christopher Reeves, Mr. Rogers, W. Mitchell, Flavia, Viktor Frankl, Helen Keller.

DAY 11: They **feel deeply and laugh often**. Laughter helps them keep things in perspective. Just as they are open to joy, they also allow tears. They show compassion for life's difficulties and use humor to help themselves and others through tough times. Examples: Carol Burnett, Bill Cosby, Anne Lamott, Alan Alda, Gilda Radner, Tom Hanks, Patch Adams.

DAY 12: They **have something they love doing** in their life. They are passionate about their work, hobbies, or sports they play and it shows. Examples: Julia Child, Suzi Orman, Dale Chihuly, Twyla Tharp, SARK, Mary Englebreit, Venus and Serena Williams.

DAY 13: They **serve a greater purpose** than themselves. They have a desire to help others and build community. They are naturally drawn to share their enthusiasm with others. Examples: Oprah, Deepak Chopra, Wayne Dyer, Cheryl Richardson, Marianne Williamson, Helen Caldicott, Norman Vincent Peale.

Enthusiastic people are like great infomercial hosts.
Even if you don't need what they're selling, you call and order it anyway.
– Mary Marcdante

Now that you know the characteristics of enthusiastic people and who personifies these qualities, take the quiz on the next page. When you're finished, score yourself to determine which characteristics are your strengths and which ones need extra attention over the next six days.

How would you rate your daily energy? (DAY 8)

1 2 3 4 5

Tired all the time...............Nap City...............Go all day...............On fire!

How curious are you? (DAY 9)

1 2 3 4 5

What life?........I get bored easily........Learning is fun........Life is amazing!

How quickly and easily can you focus on the positive? (DAY 10)

1 2 3 4 5

Life's a bitch, then you die........When necessary........Pretty quickly........In an instant

How easy is it for you to feel and express your emotions? (DAY 11)

1 2 3 4 5

I'm frozen............It's hard to open up.............Pretty easy............Tissue, please

How many activities in your life are you passionate about? (DAY 12)

1 2 3 4 5

I need a new life.......Any suggestions?.......Two and counting.......I love my life!

Are you serving a greater purpose in any of the activities you're involved in? (DAY 13)

1 2 3 4 5

I don't have time....I'm thinking about it....My family and friends....I'm a weekly volunteer

Total your score (out of a possible 30 points) and refer to the interpretation below for results and action steps.

1–12: Sounds like your internal battery has run down and you need recharging. In addition to practicing the ideas in *Living with Enthusiasm* on a 30-Day Smile Diet basis, make an appointment to see your doctor for a depression screening. There is more than enough joy to go around and it's time you had some.

13–18: What's clogging your carburetor? Is it the past? Give yourself a chance to succeed. Journal your daily successes and joys as a reminder of the good in your life. You're worth it!

19–24: You're plugging along, the gas gauge is a little more than half full, but you could use a tune-up. Are you practicing the 16-second smile every morning? Have you experimented with any of the previous day's "Tips"? Doing joy rituals daily will keep you running smoothly.

25–30: Your inner maintenance is awesome! E-mail me (mary@ marymarcdante.com) with how you do it so we can share you with the world. Your enthusiasm is the glue that holds the earth together. Keep doing whatever you're doing and share this book with someone who really needs it.

Get Out In The World and Act "As If"

These next six days feature stories and interviews with real people who personify the characteristic you'll focus on that day, followed by an action step, tips, and questions.

When you finish each day's reading, I invite you to spend the rest of the day thinking about and acting on this quality. If the characteristic is not part of your personality or daily habit, then act "as if" you already embody this quality. (Acting "as if" breaks down subconscious resistance and helps you assimilate new ideas more easily.) At the end of each day, come back to your journal and record what you learned about yourself in regard to this quality.

For example: If you are still looking for your perfect passionate work and your job isn't satisfying, when you get to Day 12, read about Julia Child and what she attributes her enthusiasm to. Then, when you go to work that day, act as if you are passionate about your job. This is a clear choice to "fake it, even if you don't *want* to make it." For just 24 hours, act "as if" you *do* love what your work requires you to do and carry out the things you think people would do if they were crazy-in-love with their work. Or, if you already love your job, choose something that you're ho-hum about – maybe it's cleaning the cat's litter box, writing that report you've been putting off, or something you really dislike doing (for me it's washing floors), then do it with reckless abandon. Smile often, and really put your heart and soul into whatever you're doing. The key is to act "as if" you love it.

Let's go on to Day 8 – Radiating Energy. When you finish reviewing Day 13, e-mail me your results at mary@ marymarcdante.com. I want to know how the days went for you. Enjoy!

I don't waste time thinking, "Am I doing it right?" I say, "Am I doing it?"
– Georgette Mosbacher

Day 8

Radiate Energy

How would you describe your energy level?

a. I go to bed wired and wake up tired. How do I get off the treadmill?

b. After two cups of espresso and a sweet roll, I'm good for about an hour and then I crash.

c. I make the energizer bunny look like a slug.

d. When I pace myself, eat healthy foods, and remember to take laugh breaks throughout the day, I can go all day.

~ ~ ~ ~ ~ ~ ~ ~ ~ ~ ~

I am always looking for great examples of enthusiastic people. When Bev Weurding, an enthusiastic friend, client, and the inspiration behind this book, calls and says, "You've got to meet this person," I jump at the opportunity. Three years ago Bev called and said, "There's a female pediatrician I met who is doing amazing things with mind/body/spirit healing. You're not going to believe her energy. You've got to meet her. Her name is Kathy Konzen."

As always, Bev was right on the mark. Kathy is as bright and inspiring as a Fourth of July fireworks display. Her energy fills a ballroom and her laughter is so infectious that she can make even the crankiest person smile. She is a wife and mother of two children, an avid runner, and pediatrician. She is also the founder of Healing Place International, a San Diego-based educational non-profit organization created to help "restore, nurture, empower and celebrate the healing spirit within."

Kathy has a deep appreciation for life and an insatiable appetite for living, in part from losing her mother to breast cancer when Kathy was 13. Because of her mother's early death and her own breast problems, Kathy chose to have a preventive double mastectomy. During her hospitalization, she had several challenges and complications. She realized during her recovery time that more than her body needed healing. "My mind, heart, and spirit also needed serious attention," she recalled. Her experience in the hospital led her to write the book, *Heading to the Hospital: 77 Tips for Getting the Most Out of Your Adventure.* It also planted the seed for Healing Place International and gave her the courage to make drastic life changes so she could pursue her true life's work. After five years of following this inner path, she had a profound two-week experience in which she was "given" her vision for the Healing Place International. From there she went into action. Her colleagues questioned her reasoning and her family worried about her future, but Kathy had learned to trust her inner knowing.

In the past two years since the idea came to her, Kathy has built an organization that includes a committed board of directors, an international advisory board, monthly gatherings that attract 50 to 100 people, and some of the best mind/body experts on the circuit teaching integrative healing techniques.

It takes tremendous energy and focus to build and sustain a volunteer organization from scratch. Kathy's enthusiasm keeps that energy flowing. When I asked Kathy where her enthusiasm came from, she said,

> I think we're all born with it. But some people lose it as they grow up. I just never did. As an adult, it helps that I'm a pediatrician. You can't be too serious with kids; they keep you in a playful mode. I can be more spontaneous and fun. Also, because of my mother's early death, I realize the preciousness of life and want to embrace it all. I see life as a wonderful mystery; and try to stay fully engaged in life so I am able to give as much as I so joyfully receive from it.

Observing Kathy over the past two years, I can also tell you that in addition to her love of laughter and spontaneity, the energy she radiates also comes from her commitment to her health and integrity, and expressing what she believes is true and important regardless of whether someone approves. There is also another factor related to Kathy's enthusiasm and that is having a sense of purpose greater than herself. Her commitment to the values of "The Healing Place" and helping people take charge of their health energizes her and anyone who comes in contact with her.

What Feeds Your Energy?

We all radiate energy in different ways, at different levels, and from difference sources. Understanding what feeds your energy will help you sustain your enthusiasm. For Janet, it's raising her four children. Susan gets energy from her daily runs before work and from gardening. Amy's volunteer work with her church keeps her enthusiasm bank account full. And for Sarah, it's sleeping eight hours a night and journaling her dreams.

Think about your life and where you get energy. Answer the statements below with the first images or thoughts that come to mind.

I get energy from ______________________________

I get energy from ______________________________

I get energy from ______________________________

Your True Energy Source Comes from Within You

How much energy we're able to radiate depends on several factors, including our individual physical, emotional, mental, social, and spiritual health. There are also factors outside of ourselves that impact our ability to radiate energy, such as the people we interact with, our work environment, the weather, and world events. In my stress management seminars, we talk about how your locus of control affects your energy and enthusiasm. While it's human nature to want to control everything, it's unrealistic and stressful to expect that you can. All you really have control over is yourself. Once you embrace this thought, your ability to radiate energy and enthusiasm increases dramatically.

Go back and look at your energy list. Notice which energy sources you have control over and which are outside of yourself. Write them in below. Your goal is to have at least three energy sources that come from within for each source outside your control.

Outside of Your Control	**Within Your Control**
____________________	____________________
____________________	____________________
____________________	____________________

Remember What It Feels Like to Be Full of Energy

Do you know what your body, mind, and spirit feel like when you have all the energy you wanted or need? Karen Rowinsky, author of *Come Alive: 50 Easy Ways to Have More Energy Now,* suggests reflecting back to a time where you felt full of energy and writing down what you were doing and a list of words that describe that experience. If you can't think of a time, choose one of the activities you listed in the "I get energy from…" exercise above. Describe what your body, mind, and spirit feel like when you're doing that activity. Sometimes, we're so tired and busy we forget what it feels like when we're at our most energized. Instead, we settle into a less-than-optimal state. Keeping your list handy through this **21-Day Smile Diet**, you will be better able to focus on the importance of doing things that give you more energy.

To get started, here's a list of sample words from Karen's book that describe an energetic state:

Body	Light, bouncy, good, free, breathe easier, comfortable, floating, tingly
Mind	Clear thinking, have good memory, optimistic, positive, resourceful, creative
Spirit	Happy-go-lucky, enthusiastic, spirited, increased sense of humor, loving, excited

Nap Your Way to Radiant Energy

Of all the complaints I hear in my programs and in conversations with friends, one of the most common is, "I'm so fatigued. I never get enough sleep." Adequate rest is a key component of radiating vibrant energy. If you have to rearrange your priorities to get more done with less time (and who doesn't?), give yourself permission to let go of other things before you give up sleep.

A 2002 survey by the National Sleep Foundation found that as many as 47 million adults may be putting themselves at risk for injury, and health and behavior problems because they aren't getting the minimum sleep needed to be fully alert the next day. Thirty-two percent of people say they get less than six hours of sleep a night during the week. And in the days after September 11, 47 percent of Americans reported difficulty sleeping at night.

What about you? Are you getting enough sleep to feel enthusiastic about your life? Would a nap help?

You may laugh (and I hope you do) but when you read the results of the research on napping below, maybe you'll become a power napper, too.

According to the Canadian paper *The Edmonton Sun*, "studies have shown that a brief nap can improve mood, alertness, judgment, creativity, concentration and boost energy. But Americans are getting 20 percent less sleep than they did at the turn of the century, and they're working under increasing stress and pressure."

Used wisely, napping is a great way to catch up on your sleep deficit and tap into alpha waves that put you at your creative best. Creativity stokes your enthusiasm and helps you get more done. The brilliant Swiss psychologist Carl Jung and physicist Albert Einstein were great nappers, using short rest periods to mine their creative unconscious for ideas and insights into problems they were attempting to solve.

Making the Most of Creative Napping

Two types of naps fuel enthusiasm: stress-releasing naps and creative naps. For a stress-release nap, set a timer with a soft ringer for 20 minutes. Slow down your breathing. Follow your breath in and out for the allotted time, maintaining a soft smile on your face to keep the endorphins flowing in your body. For a creative nap, follow these steps:

1. Find a quiet place to rest. If you are at work and if there is no lounge or quiet room, as a last resort, you know where to go. Choose the end stall if it's available.
2. Set a timer with a soft ringer and keep a pad of paper and pen next to you. (Just bring a pen if you use the restroom; you'll already have paper.)
3. Before your nap, focus your mind on one item you want to accomplish, pose a question to your mind and then let it go. (Writing out your question helps clarify what you want.)
4. Limit the length of your nap to 20 minutes.
5. Tell yourself that you will rest for the specified time and awaken relaxed and refreshed.
6. Do a deep relaxation from head to toe, breathing slowly and deeply, following your breath just like you did in the stress release nap.
7. Upon waking, record any insights or answers that pooped out during your nap.

How to Nap at Work

My mother napped a lot and enjoyed it. So did my father. I nap and feel guilty. Our "do more now in less time" culture does not support napping, although there are signs we're beginning to relent. There is actually a business called "The Napping Company." This unique company offers workshops to corporations on how to maximize productivity and safety with naps, and helps these companies set up napping rooms.

Eighty percent of the time I have the energy to go from six in the morning until eleven or twelve at night. But there are days during a long speaking tour or writing marathon that I can barely keep my eyes open. I start dreaming of stretching out on my couch and sneaking in a nap.

One afternoon several years ago I was in a business meeting. It was just after lunch and before I'd learned about eating for energy at lunch (high protein, low fat, small portions, nix the white carbs). The CEO of the company was reporting on a new product. I was sitting at a conference table with my left elbow on the table and hand propping up my chin. The room was warm and the CEO's voice was hypnotic. I found myself starting to nod off. The next thing I knew my forehead hit the top of the table with a bang and my catnap came to an abrupt halt. Later I was told my narcoleptic moment helped tighten up the CEO's speech, but I don't recommend unconsciousness as a form of feedback. Probably better to just avoid the Fettuccine Alfredo and dessert at lunch and nap for 20 minutes in the end stall of the restroom during the break.

Even God Naps

If you're still wondering if there's any real value to napping, be sure to go to the website www.napping.com. Website founder Bill Anthony, Director of the Center for Psychiatric Rehabilitation at Boston University and author of *The Art of Napping* writes, "As the Bible says, 'On the seventh day...God rested.' Even God naps!"

Today's Action Step

If you're too tired to do Option 1, try Option 2.

Option 1: Notice where you get energy and give away energy. Keep a small notebook with you, or use your PDA to record the actions, places, people, or experiences that nourish you and drain you. At the end of the day review your list. Circle the things that gave you energy. Then go back and star the things that are within your control that gave you energy. Count them up. Your goal is to have five energy-builders within your control. If you get stuck, ask a friend to help you.

Option 2: Take a nap. See the instructions on previous pages.

Tips for Creating More Enthusiasm

- ❑ Ask your company to research setting up a napping room.
- ❑ Make a list of five activities or actions you can do to give yourself more energy.
- ❑ Do jumping jacks and free-form dance in the morning for 3–5 minutes to wake up your body.
- ❑ Breathe to increase your energy. Make your inhale longer than your exhale and quickly inhale and exhale 20 times. Work up to one minute. If you start to feel lightheaded, stop and resume normal breathing. Your brain isn't used to so much oxygen all at once and needs a more gradual build-up.
- ❑ Get out in the fresh air a few times a day. Sounds simple but so many of us spend our days locked in our office in buildings that have little fresh ventilation.

Questions to Ask Yourself

- Who is the most energetic person you know? What activities does he or she do?
- What is your favorite way to create energy quickly?
- When was the last time you felt full of energy? What were you doing?
- What one thing could you do that you're not already doing that would increase your energy?
- What one thing could you stop doing that would increase your energy?

Day 9

Be Curious and Interested in Life

How many questions did you ask yourself or others yesterday?

a. *What does this question have to do with enthusiasm?*

b. *One. In a restaurant. Where's the bathroom?*

c. *At least 100 before lunch. The only dumb question is an unasked one.*

d. *I had a list of 20 for the doctor. I know from researching Alzheimer's after my dad was diagnosed that learning helps keep the brain healthy, so I commit to learning something new every day.*

~ ~ ~ ~ ~ ~ ~ ~ ~ ~ ~ ~

My Grandpa Charlie lived to be 98 years old. An inventor, he had a basement workshop full of gadgets and gizmos. When I was a young girl, I often joined my grandparents along with my cousins Judy and Bobby for Friday overnights. On Saturday mornings after we finished breakfast, Grandpa would take us down to the basement and welcome us into his magical kingdom of inventions. Inside we saw walls and walls of tools, cameras, pipes, saws, compasses, clocks, and books. I was spellbound. Our time together would include a question-and-answer session that started with him showing us an object and asking, "What do you think this does?" We'd each offer a guess, never getting it right. He'd say, "Good guess. Try again." He would continue asking us until we'd each given him at least three different answers. Then with an enthusiastic voice, he'd tell us what the purpose of the object was. I was enchanted and couldn't wait for the next visit.

After my grandmother died when I was 10, all of the precious lessons stopped, with an important exception. It was my 16th summer when I got my driver's license. By now, Grandpa was 89. He let me drive him in his big green Cadillac convertible to the Shorewood Senior Center (he called it "Senior Recess") to play cards and "meet chicks" as he once told me. During one of those drives, I asked him, "Grandpa, you're getting up there in years and, forgive me if I sound rude, but what keeps you going when Gramma and all your friends have died? You're so much fun and you still laugh a lot. Why do you think you've lived so long?" He thought about it for a while, and then said, "This is important. Pay attention. There are three rules to enjoying a long life.

"Number one – everything in moderation."

Now you can imagine, at 16, I immediately thought, "Boring!"

He continued, "Number two, be interested in life and life will always be interesting."

That caught my attention. *Be interested in life and life will always be interesting*. That sounded like a good idea. Maybe it would work with the boy I had a crush on. I promised myself I would memorize that rule.

"Number three, eat stewed prunes every morning and you'll remain regular." Oh my goodness. What an amazing guy. He was right.

Who fills the role of Grandpa Charlie in your life? Take a minute to write down the name of a person who influenced your curiosity and desire to learn. Was it a parent, relative, family friend, author of a book you read? Was it your teacher or local librarian? What one thing did you learn from that key person? If you haven't told him or her, make a point of doing so. If that person has passed on, teach the lesson to someone else.

An influential person in my life is: ______________________________

Spend More Time Playing with Children

Curiosity is a key trait of enthusiastic adults and healthy children. I heard about a study that said children ask an average of 400 questions a day and adults are lucky if they get to 10 before the end of the day. How do we rekindle that passion for wanting to learn more about ourselves and our world when we stay so busy running from activity to activity or numbing ourselves in front of the television?

For starters, if you're a parent, simply spend more time *playing* with your children instead of directing them. If you're not a parent, rent a child for a day from your neighbors or relatives, and let the kids retrain you on how to be more curious. Ask them questions about their world and how they would handle a situation instead of rushing things along and doing their thinking for them. You'll be amazed at how insightful children can be with their answers. At the very least, they'll make you smile.

> *If a child is to keep alive his inborn sense of wonder...he needs to have the companionship of at least one adult, who can share it, rediscovering with him the joy, excitement and mystery of the world we live in.*
>
> – Rachel Carson

Picnics, Pudding, and Asking The Right Question

I am the aunt of five enthusiastic boys (aged 6 to 14) whose curiosity continually delights me. And fortunately only occasionally do they annoy me when their parents are absent and they punctuate every sentence with burps, farts, and spitballs before dinner.

When Tom, the oldest, was four, he babysat *me*, as he liked to say, on a frigid morning in Wisconsin. Tom wanted to go outside for a picnic. I suggested we stay indoors, which disappointed him. Not wanting tears, I asked him, "Which room would you like to have our picnic in? You're the boss."

"The kitchen," he said, brightening up.

"Then what should we do?" I continued.

"First we'll get the blanket from the bed and put it on the floor in the kitchen. Then we'll have potato chips that are in the cupboard up there. We'll put them in a big bowl, but you'll have to get them 'cuz I'm too small to reach up there. Then get the chocolate Jell-O pudding out. You make it and I'll lick the beaters."

"Sounds like a plan," I said. Tom went to get the blanket; I got the chips and started making pudding for the first time in years. It took me back to the bitter dark chocolate pudding my mother made for me as a child, which I didn't like then. So when I noticed the only choice of pudding was dark chocolate, I said out loud, "Oh darn! It's dark chocolate. What am I going to do?"

As I was talking to myself, Tom walked back into the room carrying the blanket and said excitedly, "Wait, wait, Auntie Mary. Don't do anything. I'll be right back." He returned toting his father's flashlight and asked to stand up on the chair. He peered over the pudding, turned on the flashlight and said, "Here, Auntie Mary, now you can see the dark chocolate better."

What a scream! Whenever I'm faced with a situation that appears to have no answer, I smile and think of that moment. It helps me remember to be interested in life – whether it's encouraging a child's imagination or reviving an adult's sense of wonder – and life will always be interesting.

Never, Never Stop Asking Questions

Have you ever watched a good trial attorney turn a jury around instantaneously with just a single question? Or seen a high-performing salesperson ask the perfect question to close the deal? Or heard a story about someone who asked his or her doctor, "I'm sure it's nothing, but would you check this little mole down here?" only to find it was malignant melanoma skin cancer?

This past year as I delivered keynote presentations around the U.S. for Speaking of Women's Health events, my session always followed a videotaped introduction of Florence Henderson, best known as TV's Mrs. Brady and the national honorary chair for Speaking of Women's Health Foundation. In meeting rooms filled to capacity with a thousand women in dozens of cities, I've noticed that the room becomes as still as night and the attention of the audience becomes rapt at the exact same moment every time. When Florence says, "Never, never stop asking questions of your doctor," a hush comes over the crowd. We know it is important to do this, and yet, we avoid, we overlook, or we suppress our curiosity and intuition because we're embarrassed to ask. We've all heard the phrase, "The only dumb question is one that isn't asked." Sometimes, asking that dumb question of your doctor or yourself can save your life.

The power to question is the basis of all human progress.
– Indira Gandhi

Today's Action Step

Curiosity is a great way to handle stress. Through asking questions and attempting to understand and learn from your stress, you release its power over you and discover better options for responding to it. Think of something that is causing stress in your life. Perhaps it's a relationship with a difficult coworker, a parent's growing infirmity, an impending layoff, or a doctor visit you're avoiding. Write your specific concern in the space below.

Stressor:

____

Time yourself for one minute and write out ten different questions that relate to your stressor. You can begin them with "Who," "What," "When," "Where," "Why," "How." Examples: "How do I shift the energy of this situation?" "Who can help me?" "What don't I know yet that will help me solve this problem?"

1. ____
2. ____
3. ____
4. ____
5. ____
6. ____
7. ____
8. ____
9. ____
10. ____

Good job. Now circle the question you'd most like the answer to. Don't worry if it's something that doesn't seem to have an answer. Write the question on a 3x5 card or small piece of paper and put it in your pocket or purse. Throughout the day, whenever you think of it, take the card out and follow this process:

1. Say out loud, "Higher Power (or whatever your Source name is), here's my question: (ask your question. For example: What can I do to solve this financial crisis?). Higher Power, thank you for bringing me the answer to how I can solve this financial crisis."
2. Take the card to bed with you at night. Put it under your pillow. (I know it sounds strange. Just do it.) Before you go to sleep, repeat the process – invoke your Higher Power, read the question, then thank your Higher Power for bringing the answer in your dreams or wherever it is easiest to receive the information.
3. It doesn't matter if you believe this works or not.
4. Go to bed. Sleep well. Watch for answers in your dreams and daydreams, in the shower, at breakfast, while you're in the bookstore, driving, listening to the radio, or simply thinking.
5. Keep repeating the process and paying attention for signs until you receive the answer. One of two things will eventually happen if you keep yourself curious and interested. Either you'll get the exact answer you need, or you'll find that the question or situation shifts and you no longer need the answer to that question.
6. When you feel as if you've resolved the situation, thank your Higher Power for the answer and, if you like, begin the process again with another question.
7. If you get stuck or want to share your results, e-mail me at mary@marymarcdante.com. I'd like to hear from you.

Tips for Creating More Enthusiasm

- ❑ Ask people what the best lesson was that they learned in the past year. Make a tip sheet for yourself of the lessons you want to remember and save it in your computer.
- ❑ Keep a running list of questions to ask your doctor on your next visit.
- ❑ Pick a place on the planet you haven't been yet and know nothing about. Act as if you're going to visit there. Research the location at

the library, do an online search, call a travel agent to see what it would cost to get there, find a pen pal from that area.

- ❑ Make a list of all the hobbies and activities you've always wanted to try or that look interesting to you. Pick one and try it for 21 days. If you like it, keep going; if not, try another one until you find one you like.
- ❑ Ask yourself "helpful" questions more often. Why am I doing this? What do I *really* want? How will this help me? Is there a better, faster, more enjoyable way to do this? Is this *really* worth doing? What other questions should I be asking?

Questions to Ask Yourself

- What are the 10 most important lessons you've learned about life? From whom or what did you learn them?
- Who is the most curious person you know? The wisest? The smartest? What one thought or action does that person do that you could incorporate into your life?
- If you could travel anywhere in the world that you haven't already been to, where would you visit and why?
- Who do you want to be? What do you want? What two steps can you take today to get closer to your desired self-image and goal?
- What is one of the most memorable, helpful, or important questions you've been asked? Who asked you?

Day 10

Focus on the Good

How often do you focus on what's wrong with things, people, or situations compared to what is right?

a. Pointing out what's wrong and telling people how to fix it is my full-time job.

b. Does the word "Pollyanna" mean anything to you?

c. There's a gift in everything, if I'm willing to look for it.

d. Life has its ups and downs. So do people. I focus on what I can do. If I run into a problem, I don't dwell on it. I trust that, with everyone's help, we can find a solution.

~ ~ ~ ~ ~ ~ ~ ~ ~ ~

Of all the characteristics of enthusiastic people that have the power to change your life in an instant, "focusing on the good" is it. There is a saying that reflects the power of this truth: "One cannot be grateful and unhappy at the same time." I know this to be true from my own experience, which is backed up by research on heart intelligence by the Institute of HeartMath, on positive psychology by Martin Seligman, Ph.D., and on emotional intelligence by Daniel Goleman.

Focusing on the "good" – practicing appreciation and positive attention, looking for the gift, trusting, offering hope, and encouraging or supporting others – helps our body, mind, and spirit stay healthy. But that doesn't mean it's always easy to do. The human brain processes so much information so quickly and much of it is not pleasant. All we have to do is turn on TV, surf the Internet, listen to talk radio, or have a conversation to know it takes a concerted effort to focus on the "good."

Researchers say we have more than 60,000 thoughts a day. At least 95 percent of our thoughts are repeats and 75 percent of our thoughts are negative, according to Dr. Shad Helmstetter, author of *What Do You Say When You Talk To Yourself*. And if these statistics aren't enough to make you wonder how you get through a day with a genuine smile on your face, perhaps this will: Children hear the word "no" at least 148,000 times by age 18. If you're a parent with more than one child, think about how many times you've said the word "no." If what we most often think about and process through the day is negative, can you see why it's so important to work at staying enthusiastic?

> *Here are the two best prayers I know: "Help me, help me, help me" and "Thank you, thank you, thank you."*
>
> – Anne Lamott

As an optimist, I can't help but point out that 25 percent of our thoughts are positive, 5 percent are new and, as human beings, we have the power of individual choice. Am I suggesting we stick our heads in the sand and ignore reality? No, of course not. We live in a world of duality and paradox. We make choices based on a continuum of good/bad, pleasure/pain, big stuff/small stuff. What I am saying is that once you know what hurts, what doesn't work, or what drives you crazy, choose to focus on the good. Look for the gift, the lesson, the opportunity, or the positive action you can take in each situation.

Certainly the tragic events of September 11 provided us with an opportunity to learn firsthand about the importance and power of focusing on the "good." The outpouring of compassion, acts of kindness, and physical and financial support was overwhelming. So too were the responses of terror, despair, and rage. While these outbursts were real and understandable, we know from studies of post-traumatic stress survivors that prolonged negative responses lead to more stress. Those who go on with their lives most successfully spend more time focused on what they *can* do and what is working, rather than what they *can't* do and what isn't working. Supportive role models and positive direction help, too. My favorite example came from TV's Mr. Rogers – every child's best friend. When worried parents wondered how to help their children deal with the violent images on television after 9/11, Mr. Rogers said, "Tell them to look for the helpers."

Everyone Has a "Yes" or "No" Inside

Focusing on the "good" is a habit some of us learned in childhood. If we're raised by parents who see the world as a benevolent place with more good than bad, our world view tends to be positive and optimistic. If we're raised by parents who see the world as violent and oppressive, we will find it more difficult to keep a positive focus. But it can be done! Martin Seligman, Ph.D., in his book *Learned Optimism,* states that everyone is born with a "yes" or a "no" in his or her heart. While you can't change the past, you can learn to turn that "no" into a "yes" with the help of information and a positive support system.

Show and Tell Day

One of my earliest memories of the power of focusing on the "good" happened in Mrs. Murray's kindergarten class. It was Show and Tell Day. I had drawn a picture of my grandfather's house for my classmates. In the middle of showing my picture and telling my story, my classmate Debbie raised her hand and frantically blurted out, "Mrs. Murray, Mrs. Murray, Mary did it all wrong. She colored outside the lines."

The children started to laugh. I stood, feet frozen to the floor, eyes wide open, and fighting back tears. I will forever remember Mrs. Murray's words: "Debbie, thank you for pointing that out. Mary put a lot of effort into her drawing, didn't she, class? And didn't Mary do a wonderful job of coloring outside the lines?" She looked directly at me, smiled, and continued, "Mary, if you practice, you'll be able to color inside the lines, too. Let's all clap for Mary."

Even now I can recall feeling my quivering lower lip turn into a smile that beamed as bright as the sun. Mrs. Murray's skill in helping students focus on the "good" while acknowledging room for improvement was pivotal in developing my confidence and maintaining my enthusiasm for drawing and art.

Who was one of your early encouragers, someone who guided you to focus on the "good?"

Is it true? Is it kind? Is it helpful?
– Ken Blanchard

Look for the Gift

I am in a mastermind group with Susan Gilbert, a focus strategist and author of the award-winning inspirational book *The Land of I Can.* Within a recent two-week period, Susan's home was burglarized while she slept, her car was stolen, and the IRS audited her business. Watching her respond to these "situations" was a lesson in grace. Even one of these circumstances is enough to throw someone into the land of fear, blame, or depression. Yet Susan's ability to maintain a positive mind-set amazed me...and still does. After the audit was completed, I asked her how focusing on the "good" kept her enthusiastic during these stressful incidents. Here is what she said:

> Focusing on the good in any circumstance and being able to do so immediately is an art. With practice it can become as natural as breathing – automatic and life affirming.
>
> Two strategies really helped me through this experience. The first is believing that I create my own reality. The reality of the burglary could have been "I've been attacked. I've been violated. I've lost things that were important to me – physical things – a car, computer equipment and camera." That could be a reality. And where did I create that? I created that with my thoughts. So I could also create a different reality.
>
> I also chose to focus on the fact that I was safe and had the ability to create a safer environment. I focused on how some pre-existing problems were solved as a result of the burglary. For example, my front door had been sticking for months. I had been telling myself that it was sure to eventually lock me out. Because the burglars took my keys, I put new locks on the doors and got my front door fixed at the same time.

So where did that thought come from? It came from within me. I had the ability to create my own reality. Once I realize I can look at any situation and create what I want from it, then it's never about the circumstance and it's always about my experience of the circumstance. I make that decision.

The second strategy I used was asking myself, "Where is the gift in this?" Aren't you enthusiastic when someone gives you a gift? All of our lives, experiences are gifts – even the ones that don't feel like it at the time. Days, weeks, months, and years later, we can look back at what felt like a disaster – the death of a loved one, a lost romance, job, illness, etc. – and say, "Gee, it didn't feel like it at the time, but that situation was the best thing that ever happened to me."

I was speaking with my accountant after the audit. He said, "Susan, every small business person gets hit at least once. It's just a matter of time. Even though it came at a bad time for you, at least you can put that behind you." That was a reframe [changing the way one looks at something] and a gift. Better that it happens now than when my company becomes a multi-million dollar business.

If you don't train yourself to look for the gift, then it's not even a possibility. You just stay stuck in your past thinking, "It's a bad situation."

If you're willing to look, anything can be a gift.

(P.S. Susan's car was returned and the audit ended well.)

Make a list of three difficult "situations" in your life and identify the gift you received from each.

Situation	**Gift**
______________________________	______________________________
______________________________	______________________________
______________________________	______________________________

Bless Everyone and Everything That Represents What You Want

In *Day 2 – Oh What a Beautiful Morning*, I encouraged you to do a 16-second smile and a one-minute "smiling-thank-you" meditation upon waking. Here's another technique I learned during a visit to Hawaii many years ago. I had the good fortune to meet Serge Kahili King, a Hawaiian healer and teacher, author of *Urban Shaman,* and founder of Aloha International – a worldwide network of peacemakers. He gave me a pink booklet about the size of a business card titled the "The Aloha Spirit" that I still carry with me today. Its guiding message is this: Bless everyone and everything that represents what you want because energy flows where attention goes. Simple idea; *powerful* strategy. (We'll spend more time on specific appreciation strategies on Days 20 and 21, but until then, practice blessing the things you want – for example, if you want a new car, every time you see a model you'd like to have, say "Bless that car!") When you find yourself focusing on what's not working, become aware, breathe in and out through your heart, and say a blessing. Bless the situation, and then look for the people, objects, ideas, images, and situations that represent what you want and bless *them.*

> *Become a possibilitarian. No matter how dark things seem to be or actually are, raise your sights and see the possibilities – always see them, for they're always there.*
>
> – Dr. Norman Vincent Peale

I once heard Dr. Norman Vincent Peale, author of two classics, *The Power of Positive Thinking* and *Enthusiasm Makes the Difference,* speak at a conference. Someone in the audience asked him, "Dr. Peale, you're 92 years old. How do you stay so enthusiastic?" He said, "I have my faith, and when I go out for walks I bless everyone who passes me by. I say, 'God bless you. And God bless you. And God bless you over there.' I feel a little better about myself each time I do it." Someone then asked, "What motivates you to keep doing what you're doing?" Dr. Peale, with a twinkle in eye and not missing a beat, said, "Well, I've noticed there are still a few negative thinkers in the world. Someone's got to help them."

Today's Action Step

When you go out in the world today, practice blessing whatever catches your attention. Appreciate what works. Give compliments. Notice all the places, people, and situations that could use your good thoughts and send them a blessing.

Tips for Creating More Enthusiasm

- ❑ On your next walk, send each person you pass a blessing.
- ❑ Create a family and friends Show and Tell night. Combine it with a potluck dinner.
- ❑ Pretend you're Oprah and you're writing her closing column "What I Know For Sure" in *O* Magazine. List 10 things you know for sure that help you focus on the "good."
- ❑ Take one day and notice each time you begin to complain or get upset. Catch yourself and ask yourself, "What's good about this?" It could be that your best answer is "Could be worse. It could be…"
- ❑ Read *Learned Optimism*, by Martin Seligman, Ph.D., and *The Land of I Can, by* Susan Gilbert .

Questions to Ask Yourself

- What is one experience that surprised you by how good it turned out after the fact?
- Who is a good example for you of focusing on the "good"? What does that person do to model that quality?
- What aspect of your life could use encouragement and a change of heart? What could you say to yourself to feel better?
- What are ten things you feel grateful for?
- Who is one of your early encouragers? What can you do to let that person know the impact he or she has had on your life?

Day 11

Feel Deeply and Laugh Often

When was last time you had a really good belly laugh that brought tears to your eyes?

a. *This is a ridiculous question. What's the point?*

b. *I can't remember, maybe years ago.*

c. *Last month on* Friends.

d. *Just this morning! Good thing my legs were crossed so I didn't wet my pants. Life is so funny sometimes I can't help myself – I have to laugh.*

~ ~ ~ ~ ~ ~ ~ ~ ~ ~ ~ ~

Emotions are the driving force of our lives. Anger, fear, sadness, embarrassment, shame, confusion, passion, joy, love, gratitude – take your pick – they lead us to choices and actions that shape both our daily lives and our destiny. Once we learn how to appreciate and work with these wild horses of the heart, they can enrich our lives and keep our spirits running free.

Every time I announce that we're going to discuss the power of emotions in my stress management seminars, I notice a lot of chair movement, uncomfortable twitching and shifting of bodies, nervous smiles, and cross talk. I purposefully point this out and ask the participants why they think this is happening. The answers range from "emotions mean I'm probably not going to like what's coming" to "I was taught 'think, don't feel'" to "what are you talking about? I didn't notice anything."

Many of us grow up believing it's wrong to get angry, childish to feel scared, painful to experience sadness and, in some families and classrooms, difficult to feel joy. So we put on a "happy face," ignore what we're really feeling, and then as adults wonder why fun is fleeting and deep joy elusive.

Those who don't know how to weep with their whole heart don't know how to laugh either.

– Golda Meir

Once people realize that emotions are not right or wrong, that they are, in fact, natural mental states that result from the way we process information and can be helpful and even lifesaving, then everyone breathes a sigh of relief. When we think of emotions as traffic "yield" signs telling us to slow down and pay attention to what we're feeling, they work *for* us instead of controlling us.

If you haven't had a really good laugh lately, ask yourself when was the last time you had a really good cry.

– Mary Marcdante

The more willing you are to *fully* experience emotions as they come up, the easier they are to release and the more enthusiasm can flow into your life. Sometimes all it takes is venting with a friend or a good cry at the movies to tap into your feelings. (I have this urge to break out in song – "Feelings, nothing more than feelings…") But sometimes it's difficult, if not impossible, to access certain emotions because they evoke pain. The bad news is that everything from a blue mood to depression can result. The good news is twofold: The right therapist can help you unearth those feelings and associated memories to cultivate personal growth. And the **21-Day Smile Diet** can help you increase your joy and raise the volume on your laughter.

Ha-ha's, Ho-ho's, Tee-hee's, and Guffaws

Many years ago at a humor workshop by Mark Therrien – a gifted speaker and publisher of *BananaNose Fun Times E-newsletter* – I discovered several different types of laughs including snorts, chuckles, giggles, ha-ha's, ho-ho's, tee-hee's, hee-haws, and guffaws. I also discovered I didn't *have* any of these types of laughs; I was a "silent" laugher. Mark suggested that, somewhere along the way growing up, I must have been repeatedly silenced for being too loud and drawing too much attention to myself. "As a result," he said, "you didn't just turn down your volume; you turned it *off*. And now you can turn it back on."

My homework was to stand in front of the bathroom mirror at home and practice "ha-ha-ing" – forcing air out of my lungs while smiling and saying "ha-ha-ha-ha" for as long as I could. The idea was that eventually I would retrain my brain to cough out "ha-ha's" when I heard something funny.

I wish you could have seen me. Now YOU try it! I hope this makes you laugh. I remember feeling ridiculous at first, and then, because I felt so ridiculous, I started to laugh. One night, after several weeks of practice, I finally heard my natural laugh – my beautiful, loud, and natural laugh – and I cried. Big wet tears of joy, tears of loss, tears of gratitude, and tears of love. All those years of holding back came out of me like Niagara Falls. Today, my laughter makes my heart smile and is a welcome part of my life.

> *I have seen what a laugh can do. It can transform almost unbearable tears into something bearable, even hopeful.*
>
> – Bob Hope

As my interest in laughter grew, I read about a study conducted by researchers at Loma Linda University. The research stated that one hour of induced laughter from watching comedies significantly decreased the bad stress hormones (cortisol and adrenaline) and significantly increased the good stress hormones (endorphins and neurotransmitters). But here's the best and most fun news of all: *Fake laughter is as effective as real laughter in managing stress.*

Armed with this information and my new improved laugh, I started inviting audiences to practice fake laughing with me for 30 seconds at the end of my programs. Imagine a ballroom of 2,000 people fake laughing. It makes for such a fun three-ring circus, people can't wait to try it with their families and coworkers…unless they're humor-challenged. There are a few in this world, including type-A personalities like Sue whose story follows.

We have to laugh. Because laughter, we already know, is the first evidence of freedom.

– Rosario Castellanos

Won't You Just Try It with Me?

Sue came to my program along with several colleagues and their boss who had made their attendance mandatory. In the seminar business, we call these people hostages. They are not happy campers and make sure the speaker knows it. I reminded myself not to get caught in this particular woman's negative web. I told myself she'd be gone in a few hours, and I'd never see her again. "Let it go," I kept repeating. But I couldn't.

Sue resisted all attempts at humor, sitting with her arms crossed and a scowl on her face for most of the seven hours we were together. The few times her expression changed, I noticed that she seemed to be gritting her teeth the way chimpanzees do when they're agitated. During the 30-second laugh, I saw the person next to her elbow her and say, "Lighten up!" But she continued to resist.

At the end of the program, I made a point of thanking her for coming, hoping for a glimmer of acceptance. She looked away and said, "Yeah, sure. Whatever," turned and walked on. Whew! I've seen a chip on a shoulder, but this was the Rock of Gibraltar and I wanted to crack it. So I approached her again and asked to speak privately with her. She rolled her eyes and reluctantly complied.

I hesitated, then quietly said, "You know, I don't usually push like this. But I need to say that I see my former self in you. I didn't know how much pain I was in. I just thought, 'This is the way life has to be. I made these choices and now I have to live with them.' That was a lie. We can make new choices. I chose to lighten up and even though it's not always easy, I keep rechoosing that every day. I hope you will, too. Thank you for staying as long as you did. I know it was hard to do."

She didn't smile. She didn't say thank you. She just turned and walked away. I felt terrible. I knew I had overstepped my professional boundaries and went home wondering what had compelled me to act that way.

But sometimes, the heart knows what the mind can't understand. Three weeks later, I received a call.

Mary, this is Sue, the woman in your stress program who blew you off a few weeks ago. I just had to call and tell you what has happened since then.

I went home after the program thinking about what you said about how painful it is to be serious. You're so right. I fell asleep thinking about that and tossed and turned most of that night and the next.

On the following Saturday morning, I woke up thinking, "It wouldn't hurt to give it a try." So I got up while my husband was still sleeping. I stayed in my pajamas and went out to the living room. I turned on the TV to Saturday morning cartoons. I started the 30-second fake laugh and actually found myself laughing for real at how stupid I felt. And I felt good. And then I felt bad and started to cry. I realized I hadn't laughed like that with my husband for the last 10 years of our 20-year marriage.

After half an hour of cartoons and laughing and crying, I was feeling much better so I let out a really big hah-hah-hah. My husband, David, came stomping out of the bedroom and said, "What the hell are you doing?"

I said, "I went to this seminar the other day and this woman told us that we could all use more laughter in our lives. She said to fake laugh to get our brains thinking funny, kind of like jump-starting a car to get it running. So that's what I'm doing."

He looked at me and said, "Whatever," and turned around and started to walk out of the room.

I stopped him and said, "Wait. I just realized that you and I haven't laughed really hard together in over 10 years. Won't you just come try it with me?"

He said, "You're nuts. I'm going back to bed." He turned and started to walk back to the bedroom for the second time.

I was so embarrassed and hurt. But I remembered what you said about choices. So in this stupid nasal voice tone that I used to use with him when we first started dating, I said, "Please?"

He started to laugh and then we were both laughing and he came down and sat on the floor next to me. We fake laughed in our pajamas and watched another cartoon show together. It was magic.

Here's the most important part, though. Two hours later, we got a phone call from David's sister saying their father had died suddenly of a heart attack. Since then, it's been really stressful. I know if we hadn't had all that laughter, we would have never been able to get through this funeral and I don't know if our marriage would have made it.

Feel deeply and laugh often, whenever you can. It will help fortify you when you face tough times.

> *Something special happens when people laugh together over something genuinely funny, and not hurtful to anyone. It's like a magic rain that showers down feelings of comfort, safety and belonging to a group.*
>
> – Mary Jane Belfie

Today's Action Step

Today involves two processes. If you're in a funk or want some extra credit for personal growth (time for a 16-second smile!), do the first process. If you're feeling great, go to the second process and remember to come back to the first process when you need it. *This "Just For Now" process is one of the most powerful techniques I have ever used for identifying and releasing emotions.* I suggest you write this out in your journal and read it out loud to yourself. The more senses you involve in the process, the easier it is to clear the negativity.

Process 1:

1. Ask yourself, "What am I feeling?" Mad? Sad? Scared? Hurt? Confused? Ashamed? Guilty? Embarrassed? Wistful? (See "What Are Your Emotions Trying to Tell You?" following Process 2 for more detail.)
2. Once you identify the feeling, write out five to ten sentences that begin with "I am feeling (describe whatever emotion you're

feeling – anger, fear, sadness, etc.) because…" Let your feelings work their way up. If you feel tears coming, let yourself cry. Breathe, breathe, breathe, and stay self-aware. Here are some examples:

a. I'm feeling sad because I'm older and can't do as much.

b. I'm feeling angry because my family doesn't appreciate me.

c. I'm feeling ashamed because I let my sister-in-law down.

3. As you say the thought, bring your awareness to your heart and let yourself feel that uncomfortable feeling. Breathe slowly two to three times, exhaling the negativity. This is VERY important in releasing the emotion. When you feel the emotion lighten, breathe in a loving smile for yourself.

4. Keep your awareness at your heart level. Take a deep breath and say, "I choose to let go of the (sadness, anger, fear) *just for now.*" (Saying "just for now" helps the resistant part of you accept the change in feelings more easily. If you want to shift the energy, change the words "just for now" to "right now" throughout the exercise.)

5. Keeping your awareness at your heart, take a deep breath, and say, "What I want to feel is (happy, calm, delighted, grateful, etc.).

6. Keeping your awareness at your heart, take a deep breath, smile a 16-second eye-crinkle smile, and say, "I can choose to feel (happy, joyful, peaceful, calm, delighted, thrilled, ecstatic, grateful) *just for now."* Repeat your chosen words again with "I choose to feel…"

7. One of the things I can do that will help me feel (happy, calm, delighted, grateful) is (go for a walk, take a hot bath, deep breathe, journal, etc.).

8. *Now go DO IT.*

Process 2:

Fake laugh for 30 seconds at least three times today. Below are some suggested places to do it. If you come up with others, e-mail me at mary@marymarcdante.com and I'll add them to our online list and give you credit.

- In the mirror to start your day
- In the car driving to work (windows up if you're shy, but once you're a veteran laugher, try leaving the windows open at a stop light)
- With your children (I love doing this in classrooms. One of my friends, Linda Flores, uses it as a reward with her first-grade students.)
- With coworkers during a break
- After a difficult phone call
- Any time you feel low energy and want a boost

Tips for Creating More Enthusiasm

- ❑ To loosen up, watch a movie that you know will make you cry and laugh. When you feel tears welling up, really let yourself wail. Let your body tell you when to stop. When you feel laughter coming on, exaggerate it and enjoy the feelings.
- ❑ Get a group of friends and/or coworkers together and start a laughter club, take it to hospitals and senior centers. Visit www.worldlaughtertour.com for more ideas.
- ❑ Memorize a funny story, joke, or one-liner that makes you laugh. Become known for it. When someone you love is having a bad day, all you have to say is, "Did you hear the one about…" and they'll smile. So will you.
- ❑ Create a laughter file, bulletin board (refrigerators work, too) of funny stories, news clippings, cartoons, and funny things that happened to you. Add to it at least once a week. When you're feeling down, go through the file or visit the bulletin board.
- ❑ Buy fake animal noses or a clown's red nose and keep them in your car. Wear them while driving or any other time you need a good laugh.

Questions to Ask Yourself

- Who and/or what has touched you deeply in the past year?
- What is the most difficult emotion for you to feel? To express to others?
- Whom do you love to laugh with?
- What is one of the funniest things that has happened to you?
- What are your family's fun stories to tell? (Get them on audiotape or videotape!)

What Are Your Emotions Trying to Tell You?

Emotion	Message from Your Inner Self
Anger, frustration	I don't like this. Change it now!
Sadness, disappointment	I've experienced a loss. Help me let go. Fill me with something new.
Hurt	I'm in pain. I ache. Soothe me.
Fear, worry, doubt	I'm in danger (real or imagined). Protect me.
Guilt	I've gone against my values (or the values of someone else who is important to me). Make it right.
Embarrassment	I'm feeling self-conscious. Help me fit in.
Shame	I feel unworthy. Help me feel valuable.
Confusion	I don't know what to do. Help me get clear.
Wistful	I really want this. Please get it for me.
Surprise	I wasn't expecting this. What do I do next?
Excitement	Something great has happened or is about to happen. Tell someone!

What Are Your Emotions Trying to Tell You? (continued)

Emotion	Message from Your Inner Self
Joy	I feel happy. Stay in the moment.
Wonder, Awe	I am enchanted. Keep your attention here.
Enthusiasm	I am inspired, interested, and eager about something. Spread the word.
Passion	I am on fire with desire! Keep fanning my flame.
Love	I feel tender and connected. Help me stay this way.
Gratitude	I am blessed. Notice how precious this gift, person, experience is.
Happiness	I like this. Give me more.

Day 12

Do Something You Love

Do you have a hobby or activities you love to do and participate in daily?

a. *Too busy. I don't have time for anything but work and carting the kids around.*

b. *Does spending time with a new boyfriend count?*

c. *I finally got my horse after waiting more than a lifetime! Even mucking the stall makes me smile.*

d. *I love, love, LOVE the work I do matching "latchkey kids" with "after-school grandparents" at our community Senior Center.*

~ ~ ~ ~ ~ ~ ~ ~ ~ ~ ~

Three years ago I had the good fortune to meet Julia Child, the famous chef who, at age 90, is still doing PBS cooking specials, has written 12 cookbooks and taught millions of people that cooking can be easy and fun. At her recent book signing, I stood in line with more than 300 people for two hours. When I finally reached the front, I asked her, "How do you stay so enthusiastic, especially in difficult times?" Arms flying into the air, she responded in her characteristic, slightly off-key trill, "Wellllll, I eat well, I'm passionate about life, and I love what I do!"

What a wonderful expression of enthusiasm and a confirmation that doing something you love helps you get through challenging times. I love Julia Child! That she has lived so long with joy and has given so many people permission to release their inner chef delights me. As for me, I only cook out of necessity and prefer being an appreciative guest at my family or friends' dinner tables, especially when Annie and Christine are in charge.

These two women love to cook and entertain together. They've been friends for more than 30 years, and create birthday and holiday events that would make Julia beam. Annie is so attentive to the details of entertaining that whenever we have birthday parties at Starbucks, she brings cloth napkins for everyone.

When I asked Annie, "How do you stay so enthusiastic?" here's what she said:

> I'm always choosing to do things I love to do. If it's a lot of cooking – which can be too much work once I get into it – I'm still so happy doing something I love. Enthusiasm isn't just "Oh happy day" all the time. Sometimes it means working so hard that I feel less than enthusiastic in the moment. But afterward, it can give me the benefit of feeling very good about myself, not only because of my accomplishment but because I made another person's life better. That keeps me going.

Christine added this about her love of cooking:

> I love cooking because it's always new. There are constant surprises – and I haven't had too many failures [she laughs].
>
> There's room to play, to create. There's great satisfaction with the end result. And there's always something to share. It's never as much fun to cook for myself as it is to cook with someone else. There's synergy and collaboration. Annie takes me to a bigger place than I would go alone. We see things from two different perspectives so I come up with something that I never thought possible. It's really about sharing. It's about the love, the alchemy of it.

Annie and Christine have different reasons for enjoying cooking but they both love the feeling of satisfaction that comes from accomplishment and from offering nourishment to others. As you're about to discover, satisfaction is a key component of living with enthusiasm and loving what you do.

Do What You Love Whether or Not The Money Follows

In the early 1990s, psychologist Marsha Sinetar's best-selling book, *Do What You Love and the Money Will Follow*, was published. Boomers devoured Sinetar's message. After the financial bust of the late 1980s, they became frustrated their work wasn't providing the satisfaction or income they craved. At the same time Sinetar's book was released, another book reached best-seller status: *Flow: The Psychology of Optimal Experience* by research scientist Mihaly Csikszentmihalyi. Both books provide a different twist on the same message: Do something you love and you will increase your income and life enjoyment, *and* have better relationships, better health and higher job satisfaction. That's a big order for love to fill. But the research studies and polls deliver similar results over and over again.

Consider these results:

- Job dissatisfaction is one of the leading indicators of heart disease, according to a study done by the Massachusetts Department of Health, Education and Welfare.
- Studies conducted by the Conference Board found that only 14 percent of people loved their jobs. That's 86 percent of working Americans wishing they were somewhere else for 50 hours a week (which the Harris Poll tells us is the average workweek for most Americans). Ouch!

I hope you are among the 14 percent that love their jobs. If you are, take a moment to count your blessings and see what else can be added to your list of things you love to do. If, on the other hand, you don't like your job, then figure out what you *do* love doing. Determine how you can keep your enthusiasm flowing, even while sending out resumés and looking for a better match.

These Are a Few of My Favorite Things

In one of my favorite movies *The Sound of Music,* there is a scene in which Maria is trying to keep the Von Trapp children's spirits high. She sings *These Are A Few of My Favorite Things.* Listening to Maria sing her heart out still makes my heart soar. Now I know why: She was doing what she loved to do; she was in flow. There is nothing better than losing yourself in something you love doing.

Three Steps to Doing What You Love

What makes your heart sing? Is there something you're so excited about doing that you wake up without an alarm clock and break out in a 16-second smile naturally? Do you whistle while you work?

Here's a three-step process to help you do more of what you love:

1. Observe other people who are doing something they love and notice how you feel being around them. If you feel happy and inspired, you likely have something you love doing. If you feel jealous or bad about yourself, you may want to question if the activities you do bring you meaning and joy. Instead of feeling resentful of a friend or bad about yourself, choose to feel enthusiastic. You've just been given an opportunity to discover more of what you love. Interview people on why they love what they do and how they came to love it. Take notes. Explore your gifts and the things that bring you happiness. Discover what rouses your passion (sex counts, but it's not the only thing). Follow your joy bursts. Watch for people and situations that excite you. Look closely at the books, magazines, and movies you watch to see what repetitive themes show up. Notice what you *hate* doing and ask yourself what you'd rather do instead.

2. Choose to pay the price of falling in love with something or someone. And there's always a price, which is why so many people settle for night after night on the couch alone eating in front of the TV, or keep complaining about taking the kids to their soccer games or music lessons. Complaining may seem easier than playing a favorite sport or giving up smoking to afford singing lessons. But in the long run, whining steals your enthusiasm and robs you of energy and joy.

3. Act on that passion and "just do it." One step at a time. (See Day 18 – Act on Your Dreams.)

What you love is what you are gifted at. Only love will give you the drive to stick to something until you develop your gift.

– Barbara Sher

Love Is a Verb

People ask me if loving another person counts as "having something you love doing." My theory follows that of the Buddhist precept of loving kindness: If it brings you and others joy and doesn't increase suffering, it counts. So, yes, loving another person counts in my book. However, the caveat is to have other activities you love, too. Hard as it is to accept, people change, leave, and die. Having an activity you can do if and when a special person disappears from your life helps sustain your enthusiasm through the loss of that person and afterward.

Find Seeds of What You Love in Your Childhood

If you are still looking for something to fall in love with, or just want to add a few new activities to your list (I recommend at least 10 to get you through stressful times), consider what you felt enthusiastic about as a child. Your past holds the seeds of future pleasure.

Barbara Sher, who wrote *I Could Do Anything If I Only Knew What It Was,* helps people discover what they love doing. Her first book, *Wishcraft: How to Get What You Really Want,* was instrumental in helping me see the powerful relationship between what delighted me as a child and what I love doing as an adult. In particular, I loved playing "work" in my father's office, keeping a diary, taking walks in the park, writing book reports and reading them in class—all of which are elements of my favorite things to do today.

Leslie Charles, a two-time high school dropout and former welfare mother, raised herself up by the bootstraps to become a successful professional speaker and author (*Why is Every One So Cranky?* and *All Is Not Lost* among others). She has recently added "Internet storeowner" to her résumé. "I love this new business I'm starting," she says enthusiastically. "I always wanted to have a store. I have a picture of me at four years old in my grandmother's backyard standing in front of my make-believe store. I've got a big smile on my face as I'm stacking my goods." Would you guess that Leslie is almost 60 (and looks 15 years younger!). Her childlike exuberance and love of learning, coupled with her wisdom and compassion, make her an inspiring example of aging with enthusiasm. At a time when most people her age are winding down, Leslie is expanding her business plan and deciding what her next creative contribution will be.

Tell me, what do you plan to do with your one, wild and precious life?
– Mary Oliver

Barbara McNichol, a professional editor, attributes her love of editing to her experiences in elementary school. She says, "I knew I had something going with words when I was in the third grade. I loved spelling, writing on the board, and correcting papers for my teacher. I was Teacher's Pet and thought I was the most special person in the world."

Holly Herman, CEO of a financial institution, loves her work as a leader and coach because she is able to touch people's lives, give them hope, and recognize their gifts. Her experience as an adopted child influenced her life choices. "I felt as a child that I was especially loved because my parents went out and 'got' me," Holly says. "I help people realize there are no limitations except the ones they place on themselves. And I can show them they have the resources and ability to go beyond those limitations."

Today's Action Step

Make a list of three things you loved doing as a child and three things you love doing as an adult.

Favorite Things to Do As a Child	Favorite Things to Do As an Adult
______________________	______________________
______________________	______________________
______________________	______________________

Do you see any connections? If not, is there anything you can adapt from what you loved doing as a child and add to your "adult" list now? The more things you love doing, the more enthusiasm you'll feel about your life, your work, and your sense of who you are.

As you go about your day, ask other people, "What did you love doing as a child? What games or activities did you play? What do you love doing in your life now? Is there anything you love doing now that you can attribute to what you loved as a child?" Notice your energy expand as you ask these questions and remember to do your 16-second smile to enjoy the experience even more.

What the world really needs is more love and less paperwork.

– Pearl Bailey

Tips for Creating More Enthusiasm

- ❑ Make a list of all the things you loved to do and play as a child.
- ❑ Choose one activity or game from the list above and do or play it. If you loved to swing on swings, go to a playground and swing. If you loved fingerpainting, buy some paints and spend an hour creating. Spin the bottle? Everything is game!
- ❑ Read Julia Cameron's book *The Artist's Way* and SARK's book *Living Juicy* for ways to open your creative channels.
- ❑ Schedule regular play dates with your family and friends once a week.
- ❑ Join an improvisation class or go to a Theatre Sports comedy show.

Questions to Ask Yourself

- What did you love playing or doing as a child?
- What is the most energizing activity you've done in the past month?
- What activity or project have you wanted to start whenever you had time?
- Whom do you have the most fun with? How often do you get together?
- What is the most enjoyable job/career you've had? Why?

Day 13

Serve a Greater Purpose

What drives your enthusiasm for life?

a. My SUV! With three active kids, I couldn't live without it.

b. Party! I'll turn anything into an excuse to have a good time.

c. You mean, like, "Am I in the driver's seat of my life?"

d. The world needs all the good we can do and I'll do what I can to offer hope and encouragement wherever I can.

~ ~ ~ ~ ~ ~ ~ ~ ~ ~

Dianne Dunkelman is the founder and president of the National Speaking of Women's Health Foundation in Cincinnati, Ohio. The foundation's mission is to educate women so they can make informed decisions about their health, well-being, and personal safety. In less than seven years, the foundation has grown from one sold-out local event for 650 women to over 40 annual conferences nationwide. The conferences provide a day of pampering and education for women of all ages, ethnicities, and financial backgrounds. The success of the organization reflects the needs of today's women as well as the vital relationships between local and national sponsors including Procter & Gamble.

I have been blessed to participate as a speaker at these events and have been continually moved by the enthusiasm and gratitude the participants express for being there. I am equally inspired by Dianne's passion for helping women take control of their health.

Dianne's commitment to serve a greater purpose through women's health events had its beginning 17 years ago when her daughter Phoebe, at age 19, was in an automobile accident. Phoebe was paralyzed from the neck down. Dianne says, "I walked into Phoebe's hospital room one day and heard her arguing with a nurse saying that she knew her body better than anyone. She shouted, 'I'm going to participate in my fight for recovery.'' Phoebe has nearly fully recovered from her accident and her mother has fully embraced a woman's right to control her health.

Six years after Phoebe's accident, Dianne, also a fundraiser for arts, health, and service organizations, was hosting a fundraising cocktail party. She got involved in a conversation about the buying power of women (women make 70 percent of buying decisions) and the huge number of baby boomer women entering menopause. This led to a conversation with her doctor, who was attending the party, about what menopausal women (including herself) should do to minimize symptoms. Her doctor said that she'd already done so much for the community and was probably in between projects, so why didn't she just go shopping. Dianne recalls, "I always listen to my doctor, so I went shopping. But health insurance, of course, doesn't cover new clothes! And I still had menopausal symptoms. So I went shopping for a new doctor."

In addition to needing a new doctor, Dianne also learned she needed to become more informed about heart disease, osteoporosis, and hormone replacement therapy. She began talking with her friends and realized she could create an event that would draw women together to learn more about how to take charge of their health.

Dianne's enthusiasm for her work has attracted a committed and creative team of employees and sponsors, plus thousands of volunteers and attendees across the country. Her success in transferring a journey to recovery into serving a greater purpose has helped the team at Speaking of Women's Health extend the organization's mission across the nation.

Serving a greater purpose can be as extensive as Dianne's organization or it can be as simple as grocery shopping for your elderly neighbors or volunteering at your children's school. It's not the size of your contribution that matters; it's that you contribute in whatever way you can. A sense of purpose helps you do that.

A Sense of Purpose Defines Who You Are

In his book *The Power of Purpose*, Richard Leider defines a sense of purpose as the deepest dimension of yourself where you know who you are, where you've come from, where you're going and how to get there. He identifies five major ingredients in living with a sense of purpose:

- Purpose provides meaning for our lives.
- Purpose serves as a principle around which to organize our lives.
- Purpose rallies our strengths around that which deeply satisfies us.
- Purpose clarifies our interests and our work.
- Purpose often comes in unexpected forms and packages.

Serving a greater purpose extends beyond your own interests out to a larger community. This can include your family, workplace, religious, charitable, professional, or environmental organizations, support groups, sports teams, or your local or global community. You'll learn more about how to discover your personal purpose on Day 15. On Day 20, you'll discover how being part of something greater than yourself influences your health. Today, we'll focus on how to choose a greater purpose that feeds your enthusiasm and satisfaction.

I slept, and I dreamt that life was all joy.
I woke, and saw that life was but service.
I served, and discovered that service was joy.
– Rabindranath Tagore

While researching "Serving a Greater Purpose," I envisioned a continuum of enthusiasm. On one end are sensual, personal pleasures and on the other is altruism. Both are wonderful, valuable, and desirable, but sensual pleasures are often stimulated from something outside of oneself and disappears shortly after they're experienced. Serving a greater purpose arises from within, answers a deep spiritual calling, and sustains one through difficult times.

Sharon McFarland is CEO of Transitions for Health, a company that offers women's wellness products. In addition to having a holiday party, Sharon and her staff volunteer to buy, cook, and serve a meal for 90 men at a local shelter. Sharon says she also does this with a group of friends once a year. "It's a wonderful way to make a difference in our local community, stay connected, and have fun," she said.

Continuum of Enthusiasm

	Personal	**Altruistic**
Time	Momentary	Sustaining
Focus	External	Internal
Example 1	Shopping for new jewelry	Shopping for the poor
Example 2	Baking your favorite dessert	Baking for a charity event w/ your kids
Example 3	Playing with your dog	Visiting nursing homes with your dog
Example 4	Smiling	Helping others to smile

Look for Issues That Need "Doing"

One of the best techniques I've run across to identify how to serve a greater purpose is adapted from *The Power of Purpose.* Get your local newspaper and a magic marker or highlighting pen. Read through the entire paper and circle whatever catches your attention that needs "doing." Here are some examples:

- A child abuse case that makes you cry
- An environmental oil spill or an immigrant housing crisis that angers you
- An animal rescue that inspires you
- A gardening program for seniors or a fashion show for the physically challenged that excites you

Once you finish, go back through your markings and identify the top three things that "somebody really ought to do something about." This becomes your list from which you take action steps to serve your greater purpose now.

God calls you to the place where your deepest gladness meets the world's greater hunger.

– Frederick Buechner

Look back at your life and identify the places where you have struggled or achieved, and experienced deep pain or great joy. Use these experiences as a starting point for serving a greater purpose. My satisfying ten-year career in image consulting was birthed in the pain and humiliation I experienced during adolescence because of my gangly appearance and lack of confidence. But what actually inspired me to start my image consulting business was the enthusiasm I felt after reading a story in the paper about a woman who helped people look and feel better using color analysis (are you a "Winter, Summer, Spring, or Autumn"?). Ten years into my business, pain and joy redefined my purpose. I experienced the pain of watching my mother suffer and die from ovarian cancer. I also realized how much I loved writing and speaking to women. These experiences propelled me to shift my business and volunteer focus from helping people choose clothing and makeup to helping women choose health and joy.

The World Needs All the Good That You Can Do

One of the most inspiring people I've met – a woman who is serving a greater purpose through her music – is singer/songwriter and speaker Jana Stanfield. Fans say her music is the ideal alternative to Prozac – all the mood elevation with none of the water retention (time for a 16-second smile break!). Her music has been heard on *Oprah* and *20/20*; her song "If I Had Only Known," which has been recorded by Reba McIntire and others, has sold more than five million copies. Her CDs including "Brave Faith" and "I'm Not Lost, I'm Exploring," offer songs of hope and encouragement.

I cannot do all the good that the world needs now,
But the world needs all the good that I can do.

– Jana Stanfield

Jana says that her desire to help people comes from the struggles and disappointments she experienced in the music business. She yearned for a big break with a major recording label. "Finally," she says, "I stopped waiting for a major label to deem me worthy of living my dream, and I deemed myself worthy." When I asked Jana where she gets her enthusiasm, she said this:

> Are you familiar with the quote by Joseph Campbell – "Follow Your Bliss?" Well, the follow-up to that is "Follow your bliss by doing something you care about." I care about people who struggle to keep the faith, struggle to maintain a good attitude, and struggle to continue to believe that there's some higher plan and everything is working out exactly the way it is meant to for our greatest good. These things have always been my struggle.
>
> We get the message that if we work hard and develop our talent, we can be anything we want to be, so dream high. My dream was to be a nationally known recording artist with the sold-out shows, the buses, the jets, the touring band, and the whole nine yards. It's so disappointing to truly believe in a dream and then get to a place where I have to ask, "Okay, are you going to continue believing in that big dream or are you going for what seems possible?" And who hasn't been in that situation?
>
> After working in music promotion for four years, spending nights writing songs, and building a following for my music, I was asked to showcase for record company executives. It was a perfect night and I did my absolute best. I was sure it would lead to a record contract but at the end of the evening, none of the record companies felt that my music was something they could market at the time. It was a huge disappointment.
>
> But here is the nice turning point. I had a "Plan B." My plan was not to give up if they didn't choose me. Instead, I decided if they didn't choose me that night, I would take a little time off and enjoy my life – have a normal life for a little while instead of a driven life. I did this and discovered that I had been using the tree of life as a ladder, simply trying to get to the top instead of wandering around that tree and enjoying it for a lifetime.

It took me a year to grieve that dream and then I started asking, "What do I really care about?" I discovered I really care about using my music to help people feel better about their lives.

Four Steps to Discover and Serve Your Greater Purpose

Jana's tips for serving a greater purpose:

1. Find out what you care about. Ask yourself, "If I could change one thing in the world, what would it be? If I could change two things, what would they be? If I could change three things, what would they be?"
2. Look at ways you already contribute to the things you care about. I know people who care a lot about being good parents to their kids. They don't necessarily want an all-consuming "this is how I get ahead" job that takes all their time and passion and creativity right now. They want a job that is reliable and flexible, and pays well. The job may contribute to what they care about by giving them the opportunity to do a good job of caring for their children.
3. Have a "Plan B." If you're going to take a risk, plan for what you will do next if your dream *does* happen, and what you'll do if it *doesn't* happen based on your timetable.
4. Have fun and enjoy your life. If what you're doing doesn't also give you time to enjoy your life, rethink that choice. Have faith that there is a better choice for you, that you can find something you care about, one you enjoy doing.

Enthusiasm is Your Lighthouse

All of Jana's points speak to the power of enthusiasm to act as a lighthouse in serving a greater purpose. Enthusiasm is your beacon for how much joy you're experiencing and how much good you're doing. Each one of us has a contribution to make and a legacy to leave. Every person has someone who needs what he or she has to offer. How easily we forget this in the middle of a busy day or a crisis.

You are a precious, unrepeatable, gift to the world. Unwrap yourself. The world is waiting for you.

> *I have come to know that God can dream a bigger dream for you than you can dream for yourself. And that the whole role for your life on earth is to attach yourself to that force which is divine and let yourself be released to that.*
>
> – *Oprah Winfrey*

Today's Action Step

List three issues you care about and three things you love to do (review Day 12 if you need to).

Issues I Care Deeply About	**Three Things I Love to Do**
______________________	______________________
______________________	______________________
______________________	______________________

Ask your Higher Power to show you different situations in which any of these combinations could be used to serve your greater purpose. Pay attention, watch for bursts of enthusiasm, and let them fill your spirit. The answer lies within you.

Tips for Creating More Enthusiasm

- ❑ Review the newspaper for stories that move, touch, anger, and delight you. Make a list and choose one to explore for future work or volunteer possibilities.

- ❏ Go to the library or Amazon.com and do a subject search for a topic that interests you. Look for an autobiography or biography to read about a person who has contributed in this field. For example: Human services/Mother Teresa, Politics/Hillary Clinton or Eleanor Roosevelt, Cooking/Julia Child.
- ❏ Offer to help your neighbors set up a volunteer Neighborhood Watch group.
- ❏ Become a Girl Scout leader or a Big Sister.
- ❏ Volunteer at a local food shelter, animal rescue center, nursing home, or children's hospital.

Questions to Ask Yourself

- Whose contribution to the world inspires you and why?
- If you could change one thing in the world, what would it be?
- Where in your life have you served a greater purpose? Describe the experience.
- There's a saying, "Think globally, act locally." What global situation calls to you and how can you act on it locally?
- What one thing could you do for your neighborhood that would make you feel better about being a good neighbor?
- When was the last time you volunteered and enjoyed it? Describe the experience.

Chapter Four

The Secret to Daily Enthusiasm

Congratulations! You've completed 13 days of the smile diet, with another eight days to go. You're ready to learn a really good secret. But first, let's acknowledge and celebrate your accomplishments since our last review. This is important because too often we move on to the next project or activity in our lives before taking the time to celebrate what we've achieved. A quick review also revitalizes your new level of enthusiasm:

- ✓ You've learned where your energy comes from and how to nap for maximize energy. You know how to identify when you're at your highest energy level and recreate it.
- ✓ You've begun asking more questions of others and of your Higher Power, and you're doing more out-of-the box, childlike thinking to keep yourself in a learning mind-set.
- ✓ You've deepened your ability to feel your emotions fully and you've added the 30-second fake laugh to your toolbox of techniques for quickly raising your enthusiasm, even if things aren't going your way.
- ✓ You've improved your ability to focus on the good by understanding how you create your reality, looking for the gift in adversity, and blessing what you want.
- ✓ You've identified what you love to do and put the four steps to doing what you love into action.

- ✓ You've discovered the difference between temporary and sustained enthusiasm and how serving a greater purpose can add more meaning, significance, and enthusiasm to your life.
- ✓ You've taken daily action steps to turn the six characteristics of enthusiastic people into good habits that will keep your energy high.

Of the six characteristics, which characteristic was most helpful to you in adding more enthusiasm to your life?

- ❑ Radiate energy
- ❑ Be curious and interested in life
- ❑ Do something you love every day
- ❑ Focus on the good
- ❑ Feel deeply and laugh often
- ❑ Serve a greater purpose

Why is that characteristic so helpful?

____

____

____

Did you have any surprises or synchronistic events that happened? Describe one.

____

____

____

The Power of Positive Expectations and Synchronicity

Were you expecting anything new or different to happen to you as a result of what you've been reading so far? I hope so. Expectations are powerful indicators of what the future holds for you. Positive expectations set in motion a course that allows you to tap into your enthusiasm and access your deeper desires. Positive expectations create a path for more abundance to come your way.

Let me share an example. When I was writing Day 6 on "Enthusiasm and Enjoying," I was looking for a way to explain how you can increase your enthusiasm for an activity you've scheduled in the future. I used the example of anticipating a massage that was planned for next week. I suggested doing a 16-second smile every time you think about the activity in the days prior to doing this, but then deleted the story because of space. But because of the synchronicity that happened two days later, I'm including it here:

Sandra writes down that her favorite activity is to get a massage. After she finishes reading the action step for the day – to schedule an enjoyable activity within the next 24 hours – she goes to the phone and schedules a massage. She doesn't think she'll be able to get an appointment for at least a week, but as it turns out, she is able to get in the next day on a cancellation. She's delighted. She notices that she feels happy and takes a break to do a 16-second smile, letting herself enjoy her delight instead of moving on to the next task right away. She thinks, "This is great! I got an early appointment I didn't expect. I feel happy." Endorphins shoot through her body. By the time she gets to her massage the next day, she enjoys it even more because she's added the technique of savoring a positive expectation.

After I finished writing this example, I thought, "*I* really want a massage. I really *need* a massage." But instead of following up as I had described Sandra doing, I just kept writing, noticing every once in a while my body ached from sitting too long, and thought, "I should really get a massage."

The following day, I called my friend Ellen to go for a walk. A voice I didn't recognize answered the phone saying that Ellen was in the middle of a massage. I smiled and asked who it was. The voice said, "This is her massage therapist, Sandy."

Sandy! That's amazing! I thought. I just wrote about a woman named Sandra who gets a massage. "I need you!" I said. "How soon would you have time available for me?"

"I can see you in two days."

I made an appointment on the spot and delighted in my good fortune. Each time I thought about getting that massage, I did my 16-second smile and took a long deep breath imagining how much I was going to enjoy it. That's maximizing positive expectations.

When I finally received the massage, I told Sandy what happened. She said, "That's amazing. I've come to Ellen's home for three years and in all that time, I've never answered her phone. The only reason I did that day was because she was waiting for her daughter to call and asked me to get it."

I love the way the Universe works! If you haven't had these kinds of "coincidences," you will increase your chances of experiencing them when you create positive expectations and savor them when they pop up. Remember, energy flows where attention goes. Watch for synchronistic moments. They're out there, waiting for your attention, and Day 14 will help you find them.

The Secret to Staying Enthusiastic Every Day

You're going to love Day 14! The format is different than anything you've experienced so far or in future days. It's a special day. We'll take everything you've learned and put it into a structured routine that you can use to keep yourself inspired and enthusiastic. There will be lots of 16-second smile opportunities as well as positive self-talk, laughter, inspirational reading, energizing music, fun movement, and appreciation breaks throughout your day.

Do it every day, once a week, or whenever you need it. As we move into Days 15 to 21 and learn to keep enthusiasm alive during challenging times, you'll be glad you have a positive, light-hearted daily routine from Day 14 to build on.

> *Today well lived makes every yesterday a dream of happiness and every tomorrow a vision of hope. Look well, therefore to this day, such is the salutation of the dawn.*
>
> – The Sufi, 1200 B.C.

Day 14

Practice the Super Smiling Enthusiasm Extravaganza Daily Delight Ritual

How often do you hear yourself say "Wow," "That's amazing," or "Ohhh, that's so beautiful!"?

a. Not often enough.

b. Whenever I'm chasing tornadoes or passing a car accident.

c. Every time I look in the mirror.

d. Every day there are at least ten billion things – a sunrise, a child's laugh, the bud on a rose, my cat's purr…

~ ~ ~ ~ ~ ~ ~ ~ ~ ~ ~

Every day, you have the opportunity to make the next 24 hours great. Regardless of what is going on around you, you can choose to make the most of a situation and keep your spirits high. Some days it takes a little more effort than others and, once in a while, it takes *a lot* more effort, but it is possible. When you create a daily routine that includes spontaneity, joy, and appreciation, you're earning interest in your enthusiasm bank account that will take care of you during emotionally lean times.

The daily routine I've created for you today is called the "Super Smiling Enthusiasm Extravaganza Daily Delight Ritual." Humor me, please – I know it sounds hokey, but it is fun. And it just might bring out the playful part of you that is often suppressed by the more serious, skeptical, "I don't have time for nonsense" aspect of yourself. You'll be incorporating several of the techniques you've already learned (16-second smile, 30-second laugh, etc.) plus seven new strategies that are described below.

The Rituals You Know

- 16-Second Smile. Wake up to your smile. Any time is a good time to smile.
- 30-Second Laugh. Do this at least once a day. Fake it if you have to.
- Smiling-heart-breathing-thank-you Meditation for 1–5 minutes. You can do this with your eyes open. Try it at a stoplight or just after you hang up the phone.
- Creative Napping. Use this to solve problems and re-energize your system at the end of a workday.
- Positive Expectations. Enjoy the future by feeling excitement for it now.

Seven More Rituals to Create More Enthusiasm

1. Talk enthusiastically to yourself in the mirror. Greet yourself in the mirror, smile and say something loving to yourself such as, "You are an amazing spirit. I love you." Or try this: Smile and say, "I'm full of enthusiasm and I feel fabulous." This may be a stretch, but remember, the mind goes to work on what you tell it. Garbage in, garbage out or good in, good out; it's your choice.

In the next 10 seconds, call out as many words or phrases that inspire you, or read these words out loud to yourself with conviction and emotion. *PEACE! JOY! FREEDOM! I LOVE YOU! MY FAITH! CHILDREN! SLEEP! LAUGHTER! SUCCESS! MONEY! WORK! VACATIONS! THE OCEAN! CLEAN AIR! MUSIC! MY HEALTH!* How do you feel now? You're absolutely right – full of energy! Happy! Ready to go out and do something BIG! Don't wait for big things to move you. Your own thoughts and words can move mountains! Say them out loud. Sing them. Call yourself and leave an encouraging message on your answering machine. Keep the message in your mind all day.

2. Read an inspirational passage before you get out of bed. Even one or two pages in the morning can change your perspective on the day. Have you ever found yourself waking up too early in the morning, your mind racing with worry about your upcoming day? Or trying to fall asleep at night with thoughts of anxiety, not sugarplums, dancing in your head?

What do you do the hour before you fall asleep at night? Watch the news? Answer e-mail? Surf the web? Read a thriller? What's the first thing you do when you can't fall asleep or get back to sleep? Do you lie in bed letting your mind get the best of you? Or do you reach for a book that relaxes and soothes you into a restful dream state or inspires, delights, or motivates you to start your day early? (This is a great strategy for insomniacs.)

While I know sleep researchers say you shouldn't do anything in your bedroom but sleep or have sex, I find that a good book always gets me ready for sleep and helps me begin my day with a smile on my face. I treat myself to inspirational reading for five to 15 minutes in the early morning and the same in the late evening before bed. Why? Because it keeps my mind focused on the good. (You'll find suggestions for good inspirational books in the Resources section.)

3. Move your body to energizing music for three minutes. Crank up your stereo or strap on your Walkman and do a full-body shake to one of your favorite songs. Every culture since the beginning of time has used music to create specific moods. Perhaps you already use soothing music to relax yourself; what do you use to create more energy? What music inspires you? What songs or performers get your juices going? Tina Turner? Beethoven? The Beatles? Start your day with energizing music or any time you need a pick-up (or soothing music if you're wired).

Maintaining a flexible body is also helpful in creating enthusiasm. How often do you take stretch breaks during your day? Do you find your energy waning at times? To put more enthusiasm into your body, try the body shake. Think like a rag doll. While walking in place, shake your shoulders and your hands. Yes, you look very strange, but your body will be moving and you will be laughing – two signs of an enthusiastic person.

Use the body shake at least three times a day and you'll find yourself more relaxed and energized. Here are three routines to get you started:

- To get your energy going in the morning, turn on your favorite CD or the radio and do the body shake to one song (about three minutes). If you live with others, get them involved. You'll all be in a better mood in a few minutes. If they're not interested, do it yourself in the bathroom at home or in the restroom stall at work.

- At the end of your day, use the body shake to shrug off the tension you've accumulated through the day.
- When you want to get rid of people who make life miserable, start body shaking in front of them. (Just kidding, but wouldn't it be fun?)

4. Share appreciations at meals or meetings. Reconnect with your family and friends. Tell each person something you appreciated or something good you noticed that he or she did that day. It is easy to thank strangers who help us with groceries or let us move ahead in line at the post office when we're in a rush. But when it comes to family or coworkers, showing gratitude can be often overlooked. We have expectations and needs that we attach to people close to us. They get on our nerves so easily, we build resentments and stop giving thanks, forgetting how a simple "thank you" can melt even the stiffest resolve.

The deepest craving of the human spirit is to be appreciated.
– William James

I love sharing meals with others. My adopted family in San Diego, the Gardners, has a family ritual that I am always thrilled to be a part of. At their Friday night Shabbat dinner, after saying prayers and breaking bread, Dan, Dianne, Lilly, Max, and wonderful Grandpa Henry (until he passed away last year) go around the table and share one appreciation to each person at the table. Can you imagine if every family made this a daily ritual how much kinder our world would be?

I can live for two months on a good compliment.
– Mark Twain

You can also bring rounds of appreciation into your workplace. On Day 13, I shared the story of a bank manager who conducts appreciation meetings. I know a supervisor at a large grocery chain who selects one motivating quote every week for her staff. Every Monday, 15 checkout clerks receive a small card in an envelope with the "Quote of the Week" and a personal note of appreciation from her. It is a great morale booster and a company ritual they look forward to.

5. Practice random acts of verbal appreciation. Look for ways to acknowledge and thank people, especially strangers who appear down on their luck. I was at my local pharmacy one day waiting in the checkout line. I was feeling rushed and wishing the musty-smelling elderly woman standing in front of me would stop fumbling for her change and making excuses for why she didn't have enough money to pay for her cigarettes and gum. As I was complaining to myself, she happened to drop her change. I didn't hesitate to help her. With shame, I must admit, it wasn't because I was being a Good Samaritan; I was annoyed and wanted to move her along.

When I handed the coins to her, she looked up at me and smiled. I was stunned. Beyond her toothless grin, her blue eyes sparkled like the waters of the Caribbean on a perfect day. I gasped and without thinking, gushed, "You have the most beautiful blue eyes I've ever seen." She reached out her arms and hugged me. When she let go, she smiled, tears running down her cheeks, and said, "My husband used to tell me that all the time. Nobody's said that to me since he died 15 years ago. He said one day he'd come back and I'd know when he did. God bless you. Now I know!"

6. Create the "Ohhh Effect." Seek beauty wherever you can. Each day, find something that makes you gasp in awe at how amazing it is to be alive. Enthusiasm is born of delight, wonder, passion, curiosity, and connection – connection to yourself, to other people, and to the mystery and the majesty of life. This feeds my spirit. If I haven't had an "Ohhh Effect" in a while, I'll even go so far as to find something ordinary such as a pen and say out loud with energy and exaggeration, "This is the most amazing pen I've ever seen. I *love* that it allows me to write my thoughts down. Can you imagine the first person to discover writing on papyrus and how she must have felt to see her thoughts on paper?! Imagine all the labor it took to get this pen in my hand." You can do this wherever you are with most things, people, and situations. Try it when you're angry with someone you love, remembering all the positive things you've appreciated about him or her. It has tremendous power to shift energy.

7. Relax and appreciate your body while listening to instrumental music or a meditation tape that guides you to relaxation. Allow yourself to focus on each major body part and organ, starting at the top of your head and moving down through your body to your toes. Thank each part for doing its job and keeping you healthy.

The Super Smiling Enthusiasm Extravaganza Daily Delight Ritual

Now you're ready for the big day, a rich day filled with positive thoughts and actions. At first glance, the ritual may appear overwhelming, so be sure to read through the suggested levels of involvement and the action step that determines which level works best for you. The more you practice this ritual, the better you'll feel and the more you'll want to do it.

Morning Wake-up (20 minutes)

- 16-second smile
- 1–5 minutes of smiling/heart breathing/blessings meditation
- 1–2 pages of inspirational reading in bed
- Loving and/or enthusiastic self-talk in the bathroom mirror
- 5 minutes of stretching or yoga
- 3-minute body shake, jumping jacks (flushes the lymph glands) and/or free-form movement to your favorite music

Morning Wind-up (5 minutes)

- 16-second smile and 30-second laugh on way to work
- 3-minute call to a friend for shared appreciation and a 30-second laugh
- Create/review positive expectations and goals. One each for the day, week, month, year
- Look for something beautiful to admire – "Ohhh Factor"

Mid-Day Energizer (5 minutes)

- Shared appreciation
- 16-second smile and 30-second laugh

Noontime Energizer (5 minutes)

- Random act of appreciation and kindness
- 16-second smile and 30-second laugh

Mid-Afternoon Energizer (5 minutes)

- 16-second smile and heart breathing meditation during a brisk 10-minute walk (alone or shared with a friend)
- 3-minute body shake and dance to music

Early-Evening Revitalizer (30 minutes)

- Body shake and dance to music or take a 20-minute creative nap
- Appreciation with others at dinner – 5–10 minutes during a 15–60 minute meal
- 16-second smile and 30-second laugh

Late-Evening Reverie (20 minutes)

- 5–15 minutes of stretching or yoga
- Positive self-talk in bathroom mirror
- Inspirational reading
- Positive expectations for tomorrow
- Body relaxation with a 16-second smile
- 1-minute thank you meditation
- 16-second smile (if you're still awake)

Can I *Really* Do All of This in One Day?

You may be wondering if I actually do this every day. I certainly try to, but like you, some days are busier than others and sometimes I forget. That's why it's such a great idea to set aside one day every week or month for a mini-retreat. When you do, you'll re-energize yourself and significantly add to your enthusiasm bank account.

Next we'll cover four levels of involvement. Do what feels right for you and let go of any guilt. This day is not meant to burden you; it is about helping you add more enthusiasm to your life at whatever level works best for you. The first time you do the wake-up and late-night reverie segments, follow the order in which each technique is listed so you get the full benefit of the experience. Then feel free to experiment with what works best for you.

Level One:

- Read through the techniques and choose the ones that jump out you, the ones that your intuition is telling you most need to do. Or choose the one that sounds like the most fun. Commit to doing the technique all day long whenever you think of it. For example, if you're not already doing the 16-second smile throughout the day, commit to doing it once an hour.

Level Two:

- Choose one section of your day to focus on and do each of the techniques for that section: For example, you may not have time to do all the morning and afternoon activities, but you can do the Late-Evening Reverie.

Level Three:

- Commit to doing a full day as a mini-retreat. This is a fantastic gift to give yourself. And once you do it in its entirety, you'll be so pleased by how much energy you have, you'll want to do as much as you can each day.

Level Four:

- Share it with a close friend or a group of friends and do the day together.

May we be filled with loving kindness,
May we well and wealthy,
May we be peaceful and at ease,
May we be safe and happy.
– Adapted from a Buddhist prayer

Today's Action Step

Incorporate as many of the above tips into your day as you can. Avoid watching TV, reading the newspaper, or listening to radio news today. Just for today, walk away from gossip. Just for today, stop yourself if you begin to complain. At the very least, do the 16-second smile on the hour until you go to bed. If you have the time, schedule a day in your planner to do the entire day's activities.

Tips for Creating More Enthusiasm

- ❑ Sit in your favorite chair early in the morning or late at night when everything in the house is quiet. Put a smile on your face. Do nothing else but hold your smile and enjoy the stillness for five minutes longer than you would normally allow yourself.
- ❑ In your journal, draw a line down the middle of one page. On the left-hand side, make a list of five choices that keep you out of balance (saying yes when you want to say no, eating in front of the TV or in the car, overspending, etc.). On the right-hand side, next to each of your five items, write down one daily ritual you could do instead of the imbalanced choice. (Use the daily ritual list to help you.)
- ❑ Describe your perfect day and write it in your journal or say it into a tape recorder. Read it to yourself every day and allow your intuition to guide you toward actions that bring you closer to that experience.
- ❑ Spend one hour making choices from your heart. With each decision you make, focus your attention on your heart and ask the question, "What is the best action for me to take next?" Listen

and follow what your heart says. Regular practice will lead to more balanced, enthusiastic choices. (Visit www.heartmath.com for more information.)

❏ When you do your stretching, let yourself groan. I know it sounds strange, but it feels great and helps your body and mind relax.

Questions to Ask Yourself

- When was the last time you *gave* yourself a day *all* to yourself? What did you do?
- What will it take for you to give yourself a day (or even an hour) of spontaneity, joy, and appreciation – someone asking you what you want for your birthday? A loving friend to remind you? Achieving a goal? Giving yourself permission?
- What are three of your favorite inspirational books or passages? (Put them next to your bed.)
- What is beautiful to you? (Be specific and describe at least five different sources.)
- What are you most grateful for today? (Count five blessings.)

Chapter Five

How to Keep Enthusiasm Alive During Challenging Times

You have the opportunity to choose enthusiasm every moment of the day. For the past 14 days, you've been choosing whether or not to wake up with a 16-second smile. Yesterday, you chose how much good you could stand to give yourself in one day. How did it go? Were you excited or overwhelmed with the possibilities? Did you use any of the techniques throughout the entire day? Which techniques will you use more often?

Everything you've learned so far will help keep your enthusiasm bank account earning interest so that when tough times show up, you have extra energy to draw from. But sometimes 16-second smiles, 30-second laughs, and the "Ohhh Effect" aren't enough. You need stronger, more powerful and sustaining strategies to meet your needs and keep your enthusiasm alive.

In our last seven days together, you'll learn how to get through times of confusion, crisis, and transition. You'll be introduced to the most meaningful and life-changing principles and techniques I've worked with in my 20-plus years of being a teacher and student in the field of personal growth. You'll meet inspiring people who have overcome tremendous obstacles and hear in their own words how they kept their enthusiasm alive when faced with life-threatening or life-stretching challenges.

If you're sailing in calm waters now (which I hope you are), it doesn't mean you should stop reading. These next seven days are also "preventative." Start using these techniques *now* and when a crisis hits, instead of going into fight, flight, or freeze, you'll stay in flow. You'll know what to do in difficult situations and how to stay healthy, happy, loving, connected, creative, prosperous, and enthusiastic.

Maintaining Hope in the Midst of Despair

Enthusiasm is not just being a cheerleader or walking around in dazed delight, although that's a great start. It is also about maintaining hope when you or others are in the midst of darkness and pain. It is remembering that when it's raining, the sun will shine again and, in the meantime, you might as well sing in the rain, find the silver lining in the clouds, and jump in the puddles. You can always cry later.

Some people are very good at showing a happy face – no matter what the circumstances – and calling that enthusiasm. That is not my definition. Enthusiasm includes first acknowledging pain and then helping yourself or others mentally shift toward what is good and healing and supportive in the moment.

Yes, There's Baseball in Heaven

My friend Henry Gardner died in March of 2002. I miss him. He was 88 years old, a widower for his last 10 years, father of three children, and grandfather of five. He was also an avid tennis player, current events enthusiast, and joke-teller. Eighteen months before his death, he was diagnosed with multiple myeloma.

At a family dinner a few months before he passed away, he told this joke: "A man prayed to God asking him if there was baseball in heaven. God said, 'Good news, bad news. The good news is, yes, there's baseball in heaven. The bad news is, you're pitching tomorrow.'" Henry laughed his usual hearty laugh when he finished telling the story. We all laughed along with him. Silently, I realized that in his wonderfully unique and humorous way, Henry was modeling the power of using humor to acknowledge that this cancer could end his life sooner rather than later.

After dinner, I mentioned that I'd known him for eight years and vividly remembered his 80th birthday. He said, "Yes, this year I'll be 88. They're going to trade me in for an Oldsmobile [Olds 88 is a model of car]." He laughed and then, in a serious tone, said, "Did you know Geraldine Ferraro has the same condition – multiple myeloma? Doctors say you have two to four years. I just want it to be fast. Well, everybody's got to go some day."

I said, "I know, can you believe that! Who made those rules?!" We laughed again. And in between the laughter, we had acknowledged the reality of death.

The evening Henry died, I had the honor of being at his bedside in the hospital with his immediate family. He knew that he was within hours of death. When the rabbi arrived to say prayers, he asked Henry, "How are you?" In a quiet, raspy voice, he smiled and said, "Could be worse."

As I reflect on Henry, I am reminded again and again that what we do and say in moments of difficulty – or any moment really – can be transformative, not just for ourselves, but for others, especially when we say and do what comes from our hearts.

Enthusiasm is the language of the heart.
– Mary Marcdante

The Power of Holding Hands

Sometimes our hurt is so heavy, we simply don't know what to say. That's when enthusiasm can be as simple as just being there, holding a hand.

I experienced this firsthand in Juneau, Alaska, several years ago at one of my stress management seminars. When I'm invited to speak, I introduce myself to as many individuals as I can before my program begins. That day, as I said hello to one woman and shook her hand, she started to cry. I kept holding her hand. As the tears rolled down her cheeks, she said, "My name is Linda, and I don't know if I can stay here today."

"I don't know what has happened to you, Linda," I replied, continuing to hold her hand. "But whatever it is, I'd like to support you and I think today's program could help."

"It's just so painful, I don't think I can talk about it."

"That's fine and if and when you're ready to talk, I'm here," I said and began to pull my hand away, my eyes brimming with sympathetic tears.

She pulled my hand back holding tightly and said, "I'm ready."

We laughed through our tears and I sat down next to her, still holding her hand.

"Our supervisor registered four of us employees and herself for this seminar over a month ago," Linda explained. "Juneau's a small community. Everyone knows everyone else. We work in a child abuse center and had a rough winter with some very tough cases. We were all so excited about coming here because we knew how much we needed this. Then a week ago our supervisor committed suicide. I still can't believe it. There were no signs, no notes, no nothing. We had no idea things had become so bad for her."

I squeezed her hand again and said, "Let's take a deep breath." We did, and in that moment I became aware of how hopeless this supervisor must have felt. This is the antithesis of enthusiasm – the belief that there is no hope, no possibility, no option.

She went on, saying, "My co-workers just couldn't face being here today. But I thought it might help me feel better. If I don't make it through the day, I hope you'll understand."

"Of course. And I hope you'll stay," I said. "When you find yourself overwhelmed, just keep looking at me and I'll smile. That's my sign to you that you can get through this."

She chose to stay through the whole day. At the end, she said she was so glad she had reached out to me and that she wished her supervisor had been able to do that.

There may be someone in your life right now – a client, employee, friend, or family member – who feels as desperate as this woman's supervisor did, but you're not aware of it. Considering busy lives, need for approval or privacy, and desire to be in control – to name just a few reasons – people put on a "happy face" that hides their pain. Sometimes, simply by connecting and holding hands, your enthusiasm shows. Your energy lets another person know that, no matter how bad it gets, he or she is never alone. Keep holding hands and keep choosing enthusiasm. You make a difference.

> *This rock is more than 200,000,000 years old. That how long it will take before I give up on you.*
>
> – A Mother to Her Runaway Teenage Daughter

The Ride of Her Life

Sheri Rush discovered the healing spirit of enthusiasm while experiencing the roller-coaster ride of a life-threatening brain tumor. She was introduced to me through Pamela Maurer, one of the readers for *Living with Enthusiasm* and Marketing & Public Affairs Editorial Manager at Lehigh Valley Hospital and Health Network in Allentown, Pennsylvania. Sheri also works there as Director of Web Communications. Pamela shares this story about Sheri:

She had been getting headaches for years, her vision had recently become blurry and now she was lactating, even though she wasn't pregnant. After several tests, her doctor called with the results: "Sheri, you have meningioma, a usually benign type of brain tumor." Without a moment to react, Sheri heard a tiny gasp on the line. Her six-year-old son Tucker had been listening. "I rushed to him and found him slumped on the floor," she said. "Mommy, does it have tentacles?" he asked.

In a way, you could say her tumor did have tentacles – it was pushing on her optic nerve and pituitary gland, and wrapping around her carotid artery, putting her at risk for a stroke. Initially told the tumor was not operable, Sheri eventually found a doctor who reassured her that surgery could be done. She felt ready – until her pre-op testing. "That's when I freaked out," she said. "I just wanted to grab onto life with both hands and not let it go."

She would do just that on a trip to Disney World with Tucker before her surgery. "My great fear is roller coasters, and my son wanted to ride them all," she said. "I thought, 'If I can face this thing growing in my head, I can ride any roller coaster.'"

Grasping onto the handlebars on Space Mountain, Sheri kept thinking, "This won't last forever." By the time her son was roller coastered out, her mantra was, "Let's take on the next one!" She said, "That set my attitude for the journey I was facing. And the next step, the day of surgery, was filled with love and laughter."

She asked her anesthesiologist and nurse anesthetists to take an oath: "Have fun, have somebody stay by my side during surgery, and don't bump that tray that holds my brain," she laughs. Four hours later, Sheri awoke in the surgical intensive care unit. Her tumor was gone, her family was by her side, and the chaplain prayed with her. She was pleased they didn't cut her hair and that her nurse woke her up to watch *The Osbornes* like he promised.

Sheri's own healing spirit is strong. In her six weeks of recovery, she reconnected with herself and found a new love in making jewelry. But her most special moment was on Mother's Day, the day she promised her son she would be home. Tucker served her breakfast in bed – orange juice, jelly toast, water crackers, and Teddy Grahams.

All of us know people like Sheri, Linda, and Henry. Their stories of courage and healing, even in the face of death, remind us that we can live with enthusiasm even in challenging times, that we are all in this *together,* and that the sun *will* shine again.

It's a precious opportunity we have to be alive as human beings. It's been said that the chance of having a human life is something like being picked up as one grain of sand out of all the grains on the beach.

– Charlotte Joko Beck

Know What's Important

God comes to you and says, "It's your lucky day. I need a vacation. I've chosen you to fill in for me today to run the world. You've got 30 seconds to decide what four things to bring with you." What will you bring?

a. *Can you reschedule your plans until next week? I've got a big charity event coming up this weekend and they can't do it without me.*

b. *My family, my photo album, my cell phone, and a hot dish for God's freezer so She doesn't have to cook the night she gets back.*

c. *My cat, my jewelry, a bottle of wine and chocolate truffles.*

d. *My enthusiasm, my love, my creativity, and my health. If God needs a vacation, I'll need the best of me.*

~ ~ ~ ~ ~ ~ ~ ~ ~ ~ ~

When my nephew Michael was in third grade, he and I began planning how he would introduce me when I visited his classroom the next day. To get him started, I asked him what he thought I did as a professional speaker. With the wisdom of a nine year old, he replied, "You talk to people about what's important and help them get a life!"

I laughed and then felt myself beaming at his simple answer, which had been so challenging for me to identify for myself. I acknowledged his insight and then asked, "Michael, what's most important to you?" He paused a minute and said, "My family, my house, my dad's job, and laughing with my friends Nick and Arthur at school." I was surprised by his inclusion of "his" house and his dad's job until I remembered that his father was making a transition from full-time employee to entrepreneurial architect. In addition, my sister and her husband talked with their two boys at weekly family meetings about their family values and what was most important in life.

Love, security, laughter, learning. Core needs. Whether it's a nine-year-old boy, a 39-year-old CEO, or a 59-year-old nurse, we all have core needs that reflect the values we hold most dear. These needs and values shape how we experience life. Yet, many of us never explore or talk about these needs and values until a crisis hits, which only adds to the pain we're already feeling. It doesn't have to be that way.

Take the time now to identify and prioritize the values that are most important to you. Share them with the people you love. Rather than making choices by default, make them consciously and life will become easier, more meaningful, and more enjoyable. As you discover, talk about and act from your values, you unleash your enthusiasm, freeing yourself to create even more fulfilling experiences that match your values. Without the knowledge of what is truly important to you, life is one unconscious choice after another. This approach is unlikely to get you what you truly want and need.

> *What's the most important thing we can think about in this extraordinary moment?*
>
> – Buckminster Fuller

Here is a list of 20 common core values to help you get started. Read through the list, noting what jumps out at you, then follow the directions at the end of list.

What Is Most Important to You?

__ Adventure	Exploring the world; taking risks; embracing the unknown
__ Art & Beauty	Appreciating fine arts, culture; surrounding yourself with beauty; making art, music
__ Competence	Being the best in some area; mastering a craft or skill
__ Creativity	Using your imagination and resourcefulness to create solutions and express yourself

__ Freedom	Being independent; doing things on your own; having freedom to behave as you believe
__ Gratitude	Noticing what is good about life; blessing all past, present, and future experiences; saying thank you
__ Health	Staying well; taking care of your human system – body, emotions, mind, and spirit
__ Learning	Accumulating knowledge and understanding of that which interests you
__ Love	Connecting with family, friends, community
__ Nature	Acting as a steward for the planet; protecting natural resources; respecting the earth
__ Pleasure	Being happy and having fun, feeling good; being playful; enjoying yourself
__ Power	Controlling the situation around you; being successful; competing and winning
__ Purpose	Finding meaning in life; seeking to understand life; creating a legacy for loved ones
__ Recognition	Giving and receiving acknowledgment for who people are and what they do
__ Responsibility	Doing what's right; following through on commitments
__ Security	Feeling safe in the world; having your basic needs met
__ Self-Fulfillment	Developing yourself to full capacity; realizing your potential personally and professionally
__ Service	Contributing to the welfare of others or the planet; wanting to help with no thought of monetary gain
__ Spirituality	Having devotion to your faith; connecting to God or a Higher Power

__ Wealth	Earning a great deal of money; being able to buy whatever you want and do whatever you want
__ Work	Using your skills and talents to help produce a service or product in exchange for money; creating "right livelihood"

This list includes the primary values that allow for a well-balanced, fulfilling life. I encourage you to give yourself all the time you need to think about these values. List them in order of importance from 1 to 21 (1 = most important, 21 = least important). When you make your choices, choose what calls to your heart. This is not about what other people think or what you think you "should" do. It's about who you are at your best, what reflects your "True North."

I know this is a lot to prioritize. I was overwhelmed the first time I went through the exercise. However, it's well worth it. Also, because priorities change through different passages and phases in life, I review this list annually to see if I need to reprioritize. I recommend you do, too. Feel free to come back to the list if you don't have time right now. It's okay. There's another technique on the next page that will help you prioritize quickly. (Time for a 16-second smile!)

God, Vacations, and Values

We often spend more time planning our vacations than planning our lives. For one thing, it's more fun to do and, for another, we seem to save "serious thinking" time for that rainy day we never get to. In my *Living with Enthusiasm* workshops, to help people have more fun prioritizing values, I ask this question:

> *God comes to you and says, "It's your lucky day. I need a vacation. I've chosen you to fill in for me today to run the world. You've got 30 seconds to decide what four things to bring with you." What will you bring?*

Write your answers on the lines at the top of the next page. List the first things that come to mind. No censoring. Thirty seconds.

____________________ ____________________

____________________ ____________________

Review your list. If you're still questioning your answers, here's the flash session: There's a sudden electrical fire in your home and you have only five minutes to grab what is most important to you and run for your life. Will you still take what is on the list above? Cross off what you'd leave behind and add what you'd take instead.

Now, go back to your new list and rank the order of items from 1 to 4 (1 = most important; 4 = least important). You have now identified your top four values.

The beauty in knowing these values is that whenever you're in doubt about a decision you need to make, you simply ask yourself: Does this choice support all four of these values? If the answer is yes, it's a clear choice to make (although not necessarily easy to implement, which is why sharing your values with your support system is so helpful). If your choices do not support your values, then it's a matter of reprioritizing what is most important. Read Ellen's story below and you'll have a better sense of how to do this.

Ellen's Four Core Values

Ellen acknowledges that she lives a blessed life. Yet, she still finds herself secretly yearning and feeling guilty about it. She is a wife and mother of two young girls. She and her husband co-founded a successful company that they recently sold. She now volunteers her time for charitable causes. One of her interests has always been to entertain guests at home with her own cooking but she just can't seem to find the time. Her husband tells her, "Stop feeling guilty and hire a caterer." She tells me:

> He doesn't get it. And I'm not sure I do either. I just seem to have too much to do and not enough time to do what I really want to do. My husband and my daughters want my attention, and they deserve it. It's just that there's no time for me and I don't know what to do. Things always come up. I say I'll do something just for me. Then five people call wanting

me to help them or their organization and I've said yes before even thinking about it. It's like deciding to lose weight and as soon as you make the commitment you're invited to five parties. You know you're going to get tested. So you just give in and don't follow through on the commitment.

Ellen's challenge isn't finding time for cooking – it's about knowing what's important and making decisions based on the values that are important to her.

During a walk one day, I asked Ellen my clarifying question about what she would bring if she were filling in for God. "God comes to you and says, 'It's your lucky day. I need a vacation. I've chosen you to fill in for me today to run the world. You've got 30 seconds to decide what four things to bring with you.' What will you bring?" Things began to fall into place when Ellen answered the question. She said, "My family, my running shoes, my photo album, and my books."

"So where does cooking fit into this picture?" I asked her.

"It doesn't," she said.

"Not so fast," I replied. "Underneath all of these things you've identified is something else, something intangible, that is important to you. Your yearning for cooking may be tied into that. Let's take a look. Why are your books important to you?"

"Because I enjoy reading them."

"Ok. That's great. Anything else?"

"Because they expand my horizons. Because they take me to new places."

"Good. You've just identified two important values: enjoying your life and expanding your horizons. Let's look at the rest. What about your photo album is important to you?"

"It houses my memories and reminds me of how precious my family is to me."

"And why is that important?"

"Because I love my family."

"Great. Your memories also touch on another value – your family. Why is your family important to you?"

"Because I love them and can't imagine living without them."

"All right. Now you've identified your bottom line," I said. "When you get to the place where life is only worth living if you have particular people, things, or experiences in your life, you've gotten to your core values. There's one value left," I said. "Your running shoes. What's important to you about your running shoes?"

"I love running. It keeps me sane and healthy. I couldn't do everything I do without my health."

"Wonderful. Health is another important value. So, how does cooking fit into your core values of family, health, creating loving memories, and expanding your horizons?" I ask her.

"It doesn't," she says with disappointment in her voice.

"Not so fast," I say. "As long as it's connected to your four core values of family, health, creating loving memories, and expanding horizons, it's worth doing."

Ellen brightens and says, "Oh, so Stephen's right about the catering if it's for people other than our family! So if I cook with my daughters, and I cook healthy food, and we create new recipes and food dishes, maybe even from other countries, then cooking makes sense, right?"

"Absolutely!"

The next step is to identify if volunteering for charitable causes is the best way for Ellen to meet her core values. This takes us back to Day 13 – Serving a Greater Purpose. It may be that Ellen still chooses to volunteer, but the type of volunteering she does shifts. Instead of sitting on the board of a religious charitable foundation, she seeks out a hospital and offers to sit on their board, for example. Or she volunteers to be the committee chair for a family health fair and involves her daughters to help plan children's events.

> *When you're on purpose, life fits. Purpose inspires you to meet your challenges with courage and make your decisions with confidence.*
>
> – Mary Marcdante

Create Your Personal Purpose Statement

It's not unusual in our busy world to let day-to-day choices determine our lives and forget or avoid taking the time to define what's most important.

But the gift when you do is that once you have the value system in place from which to make your decisions, they're much easier to make. You just run every decision through the values question: Does the choice I'm making meet my values of W, X, Y, and Z?

To make your decisions even easier, consider creating a personal purpose statement. The statement includes your values, what you love to do, and the issues you care about, all of which you defined in Days 12, 13, and 15.

Here's an example of a purpose statement using Ellen's experiences:

> My purpose in life is to love my family, take care of my health, create loving memories for my family, and expand my horizons through cooking with my daughters, running, taking photographs of fun times together, and traveling with my family so that the world is a safe and loving place for families to celebrate each other.

If you'd like to write a purpose statement, fill in the blanks below, and then copy your purpose statement to a Post-it note or 3X5 card. Or create a colorful poster of images and words to keep your purpose handy when the phone rings or someone wants your time.

My purpose in life is to create, experience, and express:

____

(List your four values here)

Through

____

(List what you love to do from Day 12 – Do Something You Love)

So that

____

(List the issues you care deeply about from
Day 13 – Serve a Greater Purpose)

Our Lives Can Change in an Instant

Acting from our values not only fuels our enthusiasm for day-to-day living, it also allows us to get through difficult times. Our lives can change in an instant, but how quickly we forget until a crisis hits. Knowing and acting from our values can see us through. I received an e-mail from a colleague in the days following September 11 that really brings this point home.

Hello friends:

A friend of mine who lives in San Diego was a victim to the tragedy in NY last week Tuesday. Her 20-year-old daughter was aboard flight 93 that crashed in PA. Below please find her words to the community. She has agreed to have the message spread to the world. Please pass this along so that her daughter Deora can be remembered.

Thank you.

One Love,

Judy-Lee

Date: 9/14/01 11:28 AM

From: Debby Borza

The last few days have been tragic, not only for our country but most directly for the families that lost loved ones during the terrorist attacks of September 11. My daughter Deora was a passenger on United Flight 93 from Newark to San Francisco. She was returning home after visiting friends in New York to continue her education at Santa Clara University in Santa Clara where she was a junior.

Deora was a bright light. She was a gifted student, a wonderful friend, a kind and generous person beyond description. Where ever she went her light shined brightly leaving behind people who were empowered by who she was being. She impacted her friends. She impacted her schools. She impacted the animals at the Helen Woodward Center and the San Diego Zoo where she was a volunteer. Everywhere she went she left the world shining brightly.

As a mother, I will miss her terribly. She was my baby. My baby is gone. As an American, however, I am absolutely unwilling for her death to go unanswered. This was a young, vibrant woman who loved this country more than anyone knew. She loved her freedom. She was fiercely independent; a leader. She was the future of this country.

So here's my stand. Let this passing be the start of a new conversation that has this world work for everyone. Let us start a new conversation that is all-inclusive, that leaves no one out. Let us start a conversation that is tolerant of all people's beliefs, that includes everyone's God, that includes everyone of color, and most of all, that provides a future for all mankind to live in harmony and respect.

My daughter made a difference everywhere she went. Let this then be our call: To live our lives in such a way that makes the biggest difference possible in the lives or our fellow man, with no one left out. No one! Let her light shine brightly for all people for all time!

Debby

Sadly, tragedy, immediately clarifies what's important to us. Tragically, for some the lesson comes too late. When we know what is most important to us and we are willing to look for and accept the lesson or gift, we walk into a state of grace. Courage rushes in and replaces our fear. Our passion is ignited and we are inspired to share our truth, which brings more light and healing to the world.

At the end of our life our questions are very simple: Did I live fully? Did I love well?

– Jack Kornfield

Today's Action Step

Write out your purpose statement and spend your day imagining these are your last days on earth. How will you live? What will you do differently?

Tips for Creating More Enthusiasm

❑ Imagine you've been asked to give a commencement speech at your alma mater. Write a 250-word speech stating what you've learned about life that is most important, then ask to deliver it to your local high school or college's senior class. Or send it to your family members and ask them to do the same for you.

- ❑ Make a collage of images and words that represent your purpose statement (clip from magazines and your photo album) or print out a sign on your computer with your purpose statement. Put it on your refrigerator or a place where you'll see it often.
- ❑ Memorize your purpose statement and use it as a meditation mantra during quiet times or when you're out walking or swimming laps.
- ❑ Write a family purpose statement. Stephen Covey offers a great process to use in his book *The Seven Habits of Highly Effective Families.*
- ❑ Write your own eulogy or obituary. Share it with your family and friends or put it in an envelope in your "Important Papers" file for the future. Reread it every New Year's Eve.

Questions to Ask Yourself

- What are/were your parents' most important values?
- What single value brings you the greatest joy? Significance?
- What values do you most want your children to learn? (If you don't have children, think of the children in your life.)
- What four descriptive words would you want loved ones to say about you after you're gone?
- Who specifically do you need to share your values with?

Day 16

Choose Your Path

Your manager has just notified you that your job is being phased out in 30 days and there's no opportunity for a reassignment. What do you tell yourself?

a. I knew this would happen. If it weren't for bad luck, I'd have no luck at all. Watch, I probably won't qualify for unemployment either.

b. If this company were run by anyone who knew what they were doing, this would have never happened. I'm calling my attorney.

c. Great! I needed a vacation.

d. I wish this hadn't happened, but I know there's a gift in here somewhere. At least I have 30 days to prepare. I'll update my resume this coming week and send it out to my e-mail list next week.

~ ~ ~ ~ ~ ~ ~ ~ ~ ~ ~

Choices – big ones, little ones, unconscious ones, difficult ones, joyous ones. We make hundreds of choices every day. Many of them are habitual and seemingly inconsequential: Do I get up now or sleep an extra five minutes? Do I wear my red sweater or shocking pink blouse? Do I choose to eat this Snickers Bar or do I choose to eat this Kit Kat? (Some choices are very clear – when in doubt, choose chocolate!) With some choices, you look back years later and know they were turning points that changed the course of your life: Do I choose to stay in this job or relationship or do I choose to move on? Do I choose to withhold the truth or do I choose to tell my real feelings? Do I choose preventative surgery or do I take a wait and see approach?

Every choice adds to your enthusiasm bank account or drains it. Today you will discover how to make choices that allow you to live with more enthusiasm, what to do when you're deliberating over several choices, and how to shift your perspective to make the best choice. I invite you to walk with this thought and question today: "My life is the sum total of my choices. What am I choosing to think and do right now?"

Sometimes, your best choice in a situation may simply be your choice of attitude. I've learned Abraham Lincoln's words fit for me – "We're about as happy as we make up our minds to be." Every morning you choose whether you will be happy or sad. *It is your choice and you always have a choice.* When the circumstances are beyond your control, such as being laid off from a job, losing a loved one, or dealing with a chronic or terminal illness, how you choose to think about the situation directs *all* your future choices. This is a difficult pill for some people to swallow because it means dropping blame, excuses, denial, and victim thinking. But the rewards are tremendous: self-respect, an open and honest heart, better outcomes, and the energy to live with more enthusiasm.

When you have a choice that involves more than an attitude change, a choice that requires action and involves others, then life becomes interesting, doesn't it? You may find yourself torn between two choices, confused, and unable to take action. If this happens to you, revisit your values list and purpose statement, which will guide you in making your best choice, as it did Debra, a computer software engineer.

Debra was feeling pressured about her upcoming two-week vacation because her company was offering a class at the same time. This training would certify her for a new software program and increase her pay scale, which she really wanted. But she had hoped to spend her vacation at a family reunion. She knew it might be the last time she would see some of her elderly relatives. After reviewing the values list, she determined that her core values were health, love, pleasure, and service. She decided the salary increase would be nice if she took the class, but she'd be more fulfilled and have more enthusiasm for her job by going to the family reunion. She went to the reunion and arranged to take the class at night over a longer period of time once she returned.

One's philosophy is not best expressed in words; it is expressed in the choices one makes ... and the choices we make are ultimately our responsibility.
– Eleanor Roosevelt

Your Choices Become Your Life

Sometimes, we make a choice and it feels so right. But as time passes suddenly, we wake up one day and it feels all wrong. Finding the courage to make a new choice and act on it can require heroic effort, especially when we live in a society that prefers conformity and politically correct behavior. But we must remember that *our choices become our life*. It is only when we choose to answer to ourselves first that we able to give our best to the world.

Two weeks before her marriage ceremony, Joanne suddenly canceled her wedding. She said, "I was getting married for the wrong reasons. I'd been divorced for several years. My fiancé was a kind, gentle man who adored me. But I realized I wasn't in love with him; I was in love with him being in love with me. My turning point came when I was dining with friends who had been married a long time. I left the dinner table to make a call and when I returned they were laughing together and holding hands in a way I'd never done with my fiancé. This really struck me.

"I woke up the next morning feeling so sad about getting married. I spent the next few days thinking how I seemed to have lost my enthusiasm for the wedding. I called my friend and told her what I was feeling. Instead of telling me that everything would be fine, she said, 'Are you simply settling?' That's all it took. I knew what I needed to do. I had promised myself after my divorce that I wouldn't settle for less than I deserved. I could create a life full of love and laughter. As soon as I told my fiancé that I couldn't marry him, I felt a thick fog lift and I felt lighter than I had in months. It wasn't easy to do, but it was the right choice."

I am responsible for what happens to me.
I have choices; even if they are limited or difficult, choices do exist.
I need to take action because no one will do it for me.
– C. Leslie Charles

Finding Your Way Back

Right choices aren't always easy choices. In many situations, they are the hardest to make. They are motivated by reasons hidden deep within us that take time to surface and take the longest time to pay off. A friend e-mailed me recently, telling me that she'd made the wrong choice in moving across the country to take a new job. She wrote, "I'm looking at it as if I had been driving to a new destination, but made a wrong turn. I wasn't sure I had made a wrong turn at first, but kind of thought so. After driving for a few blocks, I knew, without doubt, that I had made a wrong turn and was now lost. I'm now in the process of finding my way back."

> *We need to teach the next generation of children from Day One that they are responsible for their lives. Mankind's greatest gift, also its greatest curse, is that we have free choice. We can make our choices built from love or from fear.*
>
> – Elisabeth Kubler-Ross

How to Move Beyond "I Don't Know"

Finding your way when you feel lost can be distracting, frightening, even overwhelming, especially when the outcomes are uncertain. When you're unclear about why you're making a particular choice or you find yourself saying, "I don't know what to do" more than once or twice, give yourself a timeout. Declare a one-hour, one-day, or one-week moratorium to give yourself time to explore the situation in more depth. In the future, when you hear yourself say, "I don't know," try one of these responses instead
:

- "I don't want to know."
- "I'm not ready to know."
- "I'm not willing to know."
- "I'm afraid to know."

These statements often acknowledge a deeper truth. They free up energy to help you deal with what's holding you back from getting on with your life, which is most often fear – fear of failure, fear of success, fear of rejection, fear of loss, fear of quitting, fear of you-name-it. Once you name the fear, it doesn't magically disappear, but it loses some of its power over you. I have one friend who even gave her fear a name: "Eloise." She talks to "Eloise" as a loving parent, reassuring this fearful part of her that whatever happens, there are choices she can make to deal with the situation successfully. Choose to acknowledge the fear and you put yourself in the driver's seat. You're in control, not the fear.

> *When I'm stuck I ask myself: Am I running? Am I hiding? Am I lying? Am I waiting?*
>
> – Beca Lewis

Seven Steps to Shift Your Perspective

Knowing how to shift your perspective is one of the best strategies you have for dealing with fear, making healthier choices, and living with enthusiasm.

One of the wisest teachers I know on how to shift perspective is Beca Lewis, author of *Living in Grace* and co-owner of The Shift Center. Beca's business is helping people apply spiritual perception to make better decisions and solve their problems quicker. Beca says:

> There is one law that always works in solving problems, regardless of the circumstances: What you perceive as reality magnifies. To put this law of perception into practice and apply it to any challenge you're facing, follow the seven steps of *Living in Grace*:
>
> 1. Be willing to do whatever it takes to change your point of view.
> 2. Become aware of what you believe now.
> 3. Understand that signs and symbols are a direct reflection of what you believe.
> 4. Learn that perception rules everything.
> 5. Shift to the highest vision of what is possible.
> 6. Walk your talk.
> 7. Celebrate with gratitude.

> I believe there is no other way to make a permanent change in your life without making a conscious choice to shift to a different perspective. I also believe that eventually we will all have to choose a spiritual perspective, so why not start now? Besides, every other point of view – even an improved point of view – is a Band-Aid. And as nice and comforting as Band-Aids are, what really gets to heart of the wound and heals it forever is spiritual perception.

Whether or not you share Beca's point of view, it is worth noting for two reasons: one, because the seven principles offer additional ways of living with more enthusiasm, and two, simply because her beliefs reflect *her* choices. So often we forget that our choices are our own to make. While we may turn over our choices to others, we must remember we are *choosing* to do so even when we think we aren't. Sometimes it is easier to say we didn't have a choice rather than owning the choice we made, but that perspective doesn't strengthen us. We become stronger, able to live with more enthusiasm, when we step up to the plate and say, "This is my choice. It may not be your choice, but it is mine, and I honor and celebrate my right to choose what is best for me."

> *Breathing in... I come home to the rich resources of my inner wisdom.*
> *Breathing out... Home is always waiting.*
>
> – Patricia Lynn Reilly

Today's Action Step

While thinking of a choice you're considering, hold a coin in your hand you can flip. Don't be so quick to skim over this one – this is not your typical coin toss. I'm not asking you to act on the outcome of the coin toss. I'm asking you to notice how you *feel* about the outcome of the coin toss. (Remember from Day 11, you learned that your feelings tell you what you want and what to do next.) Use your feelings like a weathervane; let the emotion choose your course. When you flip the coin and look at the answer, what is the first feeling you notice? Excitement, relief, anxiety, or numbness? Your feeling is a clue to your choice. Anxiety or numbness can be an indicator that it's not a good decision to move forward or you need more information before you make your choice. Excitement and relief can lead the way to a good choice.

Tips for Creating More Enthusiasm

- ❑ List 10 good choices you've made in your life
- ❑ Choose only healthy foods for one day all day – 6 vegetables and 3 fruits
- ❑ Choose to do a 16-second smile every hour on the hour for one day
- ❑ Choose to take a break from complaining for a day
- ❑ Choose one adventure you'd like to experience in the next year. Imagine you've already accomplished it and all the steps it took to get there. Set a date for when you want to complete the adventure and work backward to list the steps you need to take. Plot them on your calendar and take the next step.

Questions to Ask Yourself

- If you could choose to be anyone else on this planet, who would you choose to be?
- What is one of the most difficult choices you've made in your life? (Give yourself a lot of acknowledgment for this one!)
- What is one of the best choices you've ever made?
- What would you choose to do if you won the lottery? How would you spend your money?
- What choice will you make in the next year that would take you in a new direction?

Day 17

Renew Your Spirit

Where is your favorite place in nature to rejuvenate?

a. *Does the electric Zen mini bubbling brook on my desk count?*

b. *My garden or walking along the river with my dog on Saturday mornings.*

c. *Watching the full moon rise from the cockpit of my sailboat.*

d. *An ocean boardwalk, park bike path, or wherever there's fresh air and I can roll my wheelchair.*

~ ~ ~ ~ ~ ~ ~ ~ ~ ~ ~ ~ ~

There are many interpretations of the phrase "Renew Your Spirit." So before you go any further, I invite you to consider today's reading as an opportunity to suspend judgment and expand your awareness as well as renew your spirit so you can live with more enthusiasm. As with all other good ideas, take what works and let go of the rest. For our purposes, "Renew Your Spirit" refers to replenishing your energy so that regardless of what is going on in your life, you can greet the day with a welcoming smile, an enthusiastic heart, a vibrant body, and a fresh, open mind. How you sustain this place of well-being is as unique as your fingerprints. Perhaps it's a good night's sleep, or two or three, following days of running hard and fast. Or maybe it's noticing the smiles on a loved one's face, watching the sun rise or set, listening for laughter or to a favorite piece of music, feeling a hug or the curl of a baby's finger around your own, making love, petting your cat or dog, cooking, gardening, walking, dancing, running, praying, or attending church services. Or maybe it's something a little more esoteric such as channeling, chakra balancing, guided imagery, journaling, meditation, visualization, or yoga.

My friend Patti, a special education teacher, renews her spirit by walking her dog, saying the Prayer of St. Francis Assisi before work in the morning, and counting her blessings throughout the day. Joan, a hospice nurse, says she writes poetry and raises Japanese orchids to renew herself. After exploring many different paths, my favorite way of renewing my spirit is walking at Torrey Pines Beach here in San Diego during low tide, where I can watch dolphins leap through the waves and pelicans fly in formation. At the end of my walk, no matter what problem I brought along with me, I feel lighter and happier and more grateful for my life.

We are so blessed to have so many different ways to experience the beauty of life and connect to our life source. Whether we call it Spirit, God, Energy, Higher Power, Inner Voice, Intuition, Universe, Life, E.T.. or Bubba, our enthusiasm arises from this mystical place. Discovering how to stay connected to it is one of life's great challenges and gifts.

> *You pray in your distress and in your need; would that you might pray also in the fullness of your joy and in your days of abundance.*
>
> – Kahlil Gibran

Connect to the Stillness Within You

Researchers tell us that we're working harder than we ever have and are less satisfied with our lives than we've ever been. We're consuming more junk food, exercising less, and spending more time in front of the TV and Internet doing things that do not feed our spirit. Our confidence in world spiritual and political leaders is at an all-time low and fear of terrorism is a day-to-day part of our emotional and physical landscape. It's difficult at times to live with enthusiasm when the world around us appears to be falling apart. We seem to be making choices that diminish what Gary Zukav calls authentic power in his book *Seat of the Soul*. We are choosing to ignore the positive powerful force at the core of our being and we're suffering as a result. But by making new choices to connect to the stillness within us, we tap into the vital source of energy that is constantly available to us.

As before in this book, I urge you to make the choices now, before there's a need. Renewing your spirit on a regular basis is necessary for good health. Yet sadly, too many of us wait until we're so burned out that it takes twice as long to rejuvenate ourselves.

Don't Wait for a Crisis before Taking Care of Yourself

A crisis of some type, often in the form of an accident or illness, is the most common way that reminds to slow us down and finally touch our spirit. Dianne Gardner knows this firsthand. She is a wife, mother of two young adults, a former nurse, psychotherapist, and consultant. Five years ago, Dianne was diagnosed with a kidney disease that immediately ended her fast-paced life. What followed was a three-year time-out, which led to a new business leading spiritual retreats. Dianne says:

> When I was diagnosed with kidney disease, everything in my life suddenly stopped. For two years I spent most of my time adjusting or reacting to medication after medication including chemotherapy, which put me into complete remission. It was like living in a tailspin. Through enforced quiet and withdrawing from everything except getting well, I slowed down so much. I was truly living in the moment, not because I wanted to but because my illness forced me to. I literally lost enthusiasm for everything. I was frightened. It was during this long, difficult period that I turned to spiritual renewal. It was difficult at first. I'd spent so many years caregiving others, I'd forgotten how to take care of myself.
>
> As I began to heal, I tried other spiritual techniques to get in touch with my deeper needs. Music is number one for me, in particular, chanting music. It just clears the airwaves for me. It refreshes me. The CD *Enchanted* by Robert Gass's On Wings of Song choir is one of my favorites.
>
> I started playing cello too, which I'd always wanted to try. There's something about its tone that touches me. The cello's beautiful, passionate vibrations resonate with the bones and organs in my body. I became "one" with the instrument and this connection helped me heal. I also began journaling using Julia Cameron's book *The Artist's Way* as a guide. Writing

her "morning pages" clears the way for whatever is coming. It's very spiritual and very freeing.

When my soul is alive, when my spirit is renewed, everything looks, tastes, and smells better. Renewing my spirit gives me enthusiasm for life, sometimes in a quieter way, but it makes me appreciate everything more.

Dianne's healing work led her to an entirely different lifestyle that not only feeds her spirit but also helps others restore their own spirits.

What feeds your spirit? Describe 2-3 actions or activities that you do or would like to do.

____

____

Whoever you are, no matter how lonely, the world offers itself to your imagination, calls to you like the wild geese, harsh and exciting – over and over announcing your place in the family of things.

– Mary Oliver

Make Time for the Arts

Mary Rice, a psychotherapist who uses body/mind processes (music, guided imagery, and art) says that renewing the spirit through the arts helps maintain balance. "Many people don't think about the kind of music they listen to," she says. "As a result, they cause more stress in their lives. I hope you'll take the time to discover which music uplifts you, energizes, or relaxes you. Use quiet focused listening periods rather than just listening to it in the background as noise." She also recommends reading poetry aloud. "Poetry bypasses the mind and goes straight to the heart. The poetry of David Whyte, Hafiz, Rumi, and Mary Oliver, all speak to the deepest parts of the soul and lighten the spirit."

Meditation for Active People

Growing up Catholic during the era of Latin masses, firm discipline, and nuns left an indelible mark on my spiritual renewal. In the early grade school years before Vatican II, we started school every day by attending mass for an hour. Enforced quiet and singing in the choir were part of my daily routine. Thanks to having an aunt who is a nun, and two uncles in religious orders, by the time I reached fifth grade, I was sure I was being called by the Heavenly Father to become a novitiate in the Cloistered Carmelite Order of the Little Sisters of St. Teresa of the Flower. But when I asked to join the convent, Sr. Mary Marca, my fourth grade teacher, suggested I consider another vocation because I was "an active and talkative girl" and certainly God had other plans for me.

Forty years later, I still find it challenging to sit quietly without distraction. Imagine my delight when I discovered Thich Nhat Hanh, a Vietnamese Zen Buddhist teacher, and author of one of my favorite books, *Peace is Every Step.* He teaches meditation as an exercise in joy, smiling, and compassion, and includes walking meditation.

> Meditation is to be aware of what is going on — in our bodies, in our feelings, in our minds, and in the world. Each day 40,000 children die of hunger. The superpowers now have more than 50,000 nuclear warheads, enough to destroy our planet many times. Yet the sunrise is beautiful, and the rose that bloomed this morning along the wall is a miracle. Life is both dreadful and wonderful. To practice meditation is to be in touch with both aspects. Please do not think we must be solemn in order to meditate. In fact, to meditate well, we have to smile a lot.... Smiling means that we are ourselves, that we have sovereignty over ourselves, that we are not drowned into forgetfulness.... A smile makes you master of yourself. That is why the Buddhas and Bodhisattvas are always smiling. (Thich Nhat Hanh, *Being Peace*)

It's Good for Mommy to Take a Retreat

Deborah Kern is a mind/body expert and author of *Everyday Wellness for Women.* She says that her first experience of renewing her spirit came after she finished her doctoral program. She had pushed hard to finish it, so she decided to live on an ashram in Virginia for a month of yoga study. It was the first time she'd ever taken time for herself. After living quietly and reflectively while eating a diet of fresh organic vegetarian fare, she realized the priceless benefits of a quiet cleansing. She also understands the importance of family support and schedule coordination.

> As a wife, mother of a five year old, and stepmother of a 15 year old, it's hard for me to find time for myself. So when I create time for a personal retreat, it requires orchestration by the whole family. They have learned that it's worth it because I come back filled with so much more enthusiasm. They recognize it's good for mommy to take a retreat. Women who have people depending on them feel they can't take time for themselves but they need to! It doesn't have to be four weeks or a whole weekend. It can be an afternoon (preferably several hours) spent in real deep reflection. For maintenance, it is important to make daily time for yourself every now and then.

When I interviewed Deb over the holidays, she was at the end of an eight-day cleansing retreat. Her husband had taken the two boys on a skiing trip for a week and they were returning the next day. Deb said, "I was burned out. I love my family but I was so tired. And now I'm all cleaned out. There's no static, and I can't wait to see my family again. Talk about increased enthusiasm. Yay!"

> *Now I walk in beauty, beauty is before me, beauty is behind me, above and below me.*
>
> – Hopi Indian Chant

"Renew Your Spirit" Personal Half-Day Retreat

Personal retreat time is a wonderful way to renew your body, mind, and spirit. Below you'll find suggestions Deb and I created in an easy-to-follow three-to-four-hour program that I encourage you to do within the next 21 days.

Preparation: For the entire day, plan to eat fresh vegetables and fruits, drink fresh juices, or eat vegetable soup for all three meals. Give yourself two snacks (choose organic if possible). I make a big pot of vegetable soup and eat that throughout the day. Drink lots of water – at least eight ounces each hour (that's only one full glass). Turn off the phone ringer and let your answering machine pitch in for you. Inform your family and friends of your plans. If you're a mother, remember the phrase, "A happy mother makes for a happy family." If you have to, make a sign that you tape to your chest and back that says, "Do Not Disturb." Remain blissfully aware of the wonderful gift you're giving yourself and practice the 16-second smile throughout the entire retreat.

Hour 1:

- Walking meditation at your favorite place in nature. Focus on your breathing and use a mantra such as the words "Thank you. I am blessed." The point is to repeat a phrase that calms and strengthens you. Hold a soft smile while you're walking.
- Option: Do free-form movement (check out www.nia-nia.com for help in how to do this) to your favorite music for 30 minutes and walk for 30 minutes.

Hour 2:

- 20 minutes: Read your favorite inspirational authors or poets.
- 20 minutes: Deep breathe, meditate, or just sit quietly while listening to your favorite piece of relaxing, soul-cleansing music. A great resource is *The Miracle of Mindfulness: A Manual on Meditation* by Thich Nhat Hanh.
- 20 minutes: Journal. There are many techniques you can use. One of my favorite books on how to journal for enhanced personal growth is *Journaling for Joy* by Joyce Chapman.

Hour 3

- 15 minutes: Dry brush your skin before bathing. This helps shake loose toxins and stimulates your skin. Use 7 clockwise motions working up from your legs to your heart, and from your hands to your shoulders, and from your pelvis to throat.
- 45 minutes: Take a long bath in Epsom salts (the salts draw toxins out of your skin) and pour a few drops of your favorite essential oil

in the tub. Light one or two scented candles, if you like and play soft, relaxing music.

Hour 4

- 15 minutes: Eat something that nourishes you. Sip your juice. As you eat, chew your food slowly and taste each bite. Focus on the sensation of eating or drinking. Reflect on the texture, taste, and smell of anything you put in your mouth.
- 45 minutes: Take a nap! If you can, let yourself rest until you wake up naturally.

There are many variations to the above retreat. Don't feel locked in to doing it exactly as it is shown above. If your spirit insists on calling for something else, listen and follow what it is asking for. My friend Leslie Charles offers another type of retreat: "Indulge yourself. Sip your coffee in the morning if that is your pleasure. Nibble on a chocolate truffle for as long as you can make it last, paraffin wax your hands, cream your entire body after a long bath, and don't let anyone or anything interrupt you."

Whatever you do, the key is to discover what feeds and nourishes *your* spirit. Enjoy yourself! It's your life.

Today's Action Step

Schedule your personal retreat and follow through.

Tips for Creating More Enthusiasm

- ❑ Write a list of all the ways you have renewed or could renew your spirit. Make the list as long as you are old. Once a week, choose one activity from your list and schedule it into your planner. Add one new activity to the list every year for your birthday.
- ❑ Visit www.beliefnet.com and sign up for their daily inspiring quotation. This is one of the best websites I've found for staying in touch with your spirit.
- ❑ Write your own personal 10 commandments for honoring your spirit.

❏ Join or start a weekly or monthly women's spirituality group.
❏ Create a meditation tape of your favorite prayers, sayings, and music. Take a yoga or meditation class and learn how to breathe for increased relaxation.

Questions to Ask Yourself

- When was the last time you felt your spirit soar? What were you doing?
- What activity most feeds your soul? When will you do it again?
- What pieces of music most connect you to your spirit?
- Who is a spiritual mentor for you? What about them inspires you? (If you don't have anyone, who could you ask to guide you?)
- What spiritual adventure, program, or retreat would you like to experience in the next year? (Visit www.eomega.org for ideas)

Day 18

Act on Your Dreams

What dream or goal are you most excited about making happen this coming year?

a. *Why bother? Nothing ever turns out the way I wanted anyway.*

b. *I'll have to let you know. I have to check with my husband first.*

c. *I need help. How do I choose the best one? There are so many good ones!*

d. *I have two. One just for me and one with my family. I'm taking an Italian cooking class at the local community college with two friends – we're going to open a restaurant in three years. The other dream is organizing a family reunion for this summer.*

~ ~ ~ ~ ~ ~ ~ ~ ~ ~

Have you ever had a dream so big, so overwhelming, so seemingly out of reach that all you did was dream about it instead of do something about it? Today we're going to focus on moving closer to the dream that calls to you and using your enthusiasm to guide you toward the next step. There's an inspiring quotation by Goethe that I keep by my bedside. It reminds me that anything is possible if you hold your vision, commit to it, and let the Universe help you one step at a time.

> *Whatever you can do, or dream you can, begin it! Boldness has genius, power and magic in it. Begin it now!*
>
> – Goethe

What is one of the dreams you hold on to but have yet to take any action? Describe it below.

____

____

What one step you could take today to bring that dream closer to reality?

____

Wake Up Calls

One of my dreams in my late 20s was to live in a warm climate and travel the world speaking to women about how to discover their best, make healthier choices, and realize their dreams. I'd started an image consulting business and felt I was on my way, but the warm-climate dream was more than a stretch. I was firmly planted in Milwaukee, Wisconsin, living in a community filled with bright, creative, inspiring friends, growing my business, walking in beautiful parks, enjoying a strong arts culture, and eating great food at ethnic festivals at the shore of Lake Michigan.

My only complaint about life was that I was a warm-weather body living in a mostly cold and snow-filled or rainy climate, suffering from headaches, low-grade depression, and little motivation to exercise except on sunny, warm days. At least that *was* me, until the year my mother died from ovarian cancer. Her death was a wake-up call that I had to take better care of myself regardless of the weather. This was also the year that I began speaking at national conferences. In a three-week period during the month of February, I traveled to San Diego, San Antonio, and Hawaii. I was living this Oliver Wendell Holmes quote:

> *A mind once stretched by a new idea never regains its original dimensions.*

I Want That!

By the time I returned from Hawaii, I had experienced bliss and wanted to move there. My audience members were excited to hear me speak. The balmy weather, the shining sun, and the scent of plumeria trees wafting through the air as I walked along beaches and tropical rain forests enchanted me. I remember arriving in my hotel room that first night. A live peacock, tail feathers in full array, was standing guard outside my door. My room was filled with fresh flowers and chocolate. When I walked out to the balcony, a full moon was rising over the ocean. I was a giddy girl again, jumping up and down at my good fortune and writing in my journal that night, *Hawaii is the earth's manifestation of the human potential realized. Most people will never experience this exquisite beauty and I'm standing in the midst of it. How did I get so lucky?*

I got that lucky because I'd followed a burst of joyful energy several years earlier when I'd seen photos of a colleague who had spoken in Hawaii. The photos were spectacular, showing him at this magnificent resort, speaking to a thousand people and, during off hours, walking on the beach and swimming in the ocean. I laughingly but earnestly said to him "I want that!" I began to imagine myself in the photos replacing him. Anytime I heard of people speaking or vacationing in Hawaii, I asked them to take notes. When they returned, I had them describe their experience in full detail. I didn't know it at the time, but my enthusiasm for experiencing Hawaii was collecting emotional energy like a magnet that pulled all sorts of Hawaii-related "synchronicities" toward me. How else could I explain two more trips to Hawaii within the next nine months, without any effort on my part to plan them?

DREAMING + CURIOSITY + ENTHUSIASM = POSITIVE RESULT

Enthusiasm Travels with Tingles, Thrill Bumps, and Joy Bursts

I'm often immediately clear about what I *don't* want but much less clear about what I *do* want. Perhaps you've discovered this about yourself. I think this is common for many women: We are so busy caring for other's needs, we forget or dismiss our own. These "wants" lie buried in our hearts, waiting for someone or something to come along and release them, when what is really needed is for us to liberate them ourselves. This is where enthusiasm comes in.

> *Noticing when enthusiasm arrives is one of the most overlooked signs in taking the next step toward any dream or goal you're working on.*
>
> – Mary Marcdante

There *is* boldness, genius, magic, and the seed of a dream-come-true in that "joy burst" moment, waiting to be planted, tended, and grown by you. Pay attention: *When you feel a burst of energy that makes your whole body tingle or gives you "thrill" bumps, stop and acknowledge to yourself what just happened.* Enjoy the feelings for as long as you can (and then a second longer) and then ask the Universe (or your inner Wise Woman, or God, or wherever you derive your source of inspiration) for the next step. Watch for that step. It will arrive, sometimes packaged in a way that doesn't make sense or that you almost miss. But you will know it's the next step because your enthusiasm will bubble up and you'll have a joy burst.

Describe an experience when you felt tingles, thrill bumps, or joy bursts. (If you can't remember, it's time to ask your Source for one.)

____

____

Where did the experience lead you? Was it the beginning of a new adventure? Was it something that you'd like to follow up on now?

____

____

> *Every day I push away all self-doubt and replace it with self-trust. I constantly remind myself my life is unfolding in a perfect way. I trust the grand design.*
>
> – Susan Jeffers

On my third business trip to Hawaii, I made plans to move there, only to return to Milwaukee and discover that I couldn't in good conscience leave my mother as ill as she was. I was terribly disappointed, and wondered why the Universe had let me down. It had felt so right for so many months. What was the message? I resigned myself to staying with Mom until her death and reopening the door at a later date if it felt right.

That date came a year later. A colleague of mine, Paul Radde, called from the East Coast and asked, "How's your move going?"

"Not very well," I lamented. "I'm emotionally stuck. I was all set to move to Hawaii and I got the wind knocked out of my sails with Mom's death. Since then my father's had a stroke. And without any children of my own, I just can't imagine being so far away and not being around to watch my nephews grow up. San Diego was an option, but things didn't work out. I'll just take a vacation some place warm once a year in the winter. I'll be fine."

"Listen to you!" he said. "You teach this stuff and you're not walking your talk. You want to do it but you're afraid, so you're willing to settle for less. Commit to something else, but don't make excuses and settle. Get off the fence one way or the other. Once you do, the Universe will open up and say yes. If it's not right, it won't happen. But if you never try, you'll never know. By the way, why don't you call Lael Jackson in San Diego? She's a speaker. She'd help you."

"Sure," I said, knowing I probably wouldn't make the call.

Oh, that conversation with Paul was painful. He was right. Truth be told, I was scared to make that big of a move by myself. I got off the phone and walked past the dining room table. On it was sitting a three-week-old *San Diego Reader* I'd sent away for on a lark, just to get a sense of the city before I'd given up on moving there. I heard in my mind, "Call four rental ads in the paper." I was taken aback. The message was so clear. I laughed and kept walking over to the TV, but the voice repeated, "Call four rental ads in the paper." I'd learned to pay attention to this voice, because when I failed to heed, I regretted it later.

I picked up the paper, opened it to the classified ads, closed my eyes, pointed to four different ads, and circled them. I felt foolish and scared, but also excited. My heart was racing as I called each of them. Three of them told me that their rooms had been rented weeks earlier and besides, they wouldn't rent to someone who didn't currently live in the area. I left a message for one person and received a call back that evening.

"Hi, I'm responding to your call. I have a room available in my home June 15."

My brain went to monkey mind, thinking "June 15! That's less than a month away. How could I possibly close up my business and move by then? Why do I bother?!"

The voice continued, "My name is Lael Jackson."

"Lael Jackson! Oh my goodness. Are you a professional speaker?"

"Yes."

"Were you at the 1987 National Speaker's Association Convention on the Board of Directors?

"Yes."

"I met you there! After you finished speaking, I came up to you and said, 'I admire you,' and you said, 'If you're ever in San Diego, please call.' Paul Radde, our mutual friend, told me to call you this morning, but I actually called you off a blind ad in the *Reader*!"

"WHO ARE YOU?" she asked with surprise.

I explained my interest and myself and the next words out of her mouth were "Just come."

Three days later, I flew out there and three weeks later, I was driving myself across the country moving to San Diego. The rest of the story is that the Hawaii business I was going to be involved in dissolved within three months. Then a colleague I met in San Diego shortly after my move linked me with a client who sent me around the world on a speaking tour. I had realized my dreams!

I won't pretend I understand exactly how all these events lined up the way they did, especially when the move to Hawaii fell through. But I will tell you I believe that enthusiasm is more than showing excitement. I believe enthusiasm is also a gift from your Higher Power directing and guiding you toward your life's purpose *now*.

The world is not at a loss for people who dream. It is at a loss for people who act on their dreams. Take that leap of faith now.

– Dr. Discovery – John Kalpus

Today's Action Step

Watch for moments of tingling, thrill bumps, or joy bursts. Notice how many you have (or don't have). If you haven't experienced one of these joy-filled moments by noon, it's time to seek one out. Expect that one is waiting for you! Ask your intuition for one before you go to bed. E-mail me tomorrow and let me know what happened: mary@ marymarcdante.com

Tips for Creating More Enthusiasm

- ❑ Make a list of ten tingles, thrill bumps, or joy bursts you've had and look for the common thread. Your purpose is woven in between them.
- ❑ Notice when what you're doing seems effortless and light-hearted. Keep a list of these experiences and use it to follow the best path.
- ❑ When you feel a strong urge to follow an idea, *take action*! When you listen to your intuition and act on it, it will reward you with experiences you never dreamed possible!
- ❑ Find a dream buddy. Join the Dream Big! Club together and support each other's dreams. Contact Barbara Sanfilippo, author of *Dream Big! What's the Best That Could Happen?* at www.romanosanfilippo.com.
- ❑ Make a list of 100 experiences you want to have before you die.

Questions to Ask Yourself

- What is one dream come true you experienced as a child?
- How does your body show you the next step to reach a goal or dream? Does your body give you tingles? Thrill bumps? Joy bursts? Something else?
- Whom do you know who has realized a dream that got your attention? What did they do? (Look for seeds to your dream in *their* dreams.)
- What have you wished for and are still waiting to come to you?
- What one step do you need to take to help that wish come true?

Day 19

Let Go and Live in the Moment

How many people are you avoiding or not speaking to because of a past unpleasant experience with them?

a. *My lawyer said to plead the Fifth.*

b. *My therapist says, "If you have to ask the answer is 'yes.'"*

c. *None. I hate conflict and confrontation, so I make sure I never get that close to anyone, or I keep my mouth shut and look the other way.*

d. *None. I can't control the past but I can control my thinking. When I encounter uncomfortable situations, I either deal with them directly or address them as soon as possible. I also keep working on forgiving. It's a daily process but the peace of mind is worth it.*

~ ~ ~ ~ ~ ~ ~ ~ ~ ~ ~ ~

The voice mail message said she was sorry she missed my call. She had just returned from caring for her dearest friend of 30 years who had breast cancer. I hadn't talked to Kathi Ingersoll since first meeting her at a conference where I'd spoken two years ago, but I had carried her in my heart since then. Her life story had profoundly touched me and reminded me again of how powerful is to declare, as she did, "Let go and live on!"

Kathi had approached me at the cocktail party following my speech and asked if we could talk. She said that following my presentation she went straight to the phone and called her sister. They hadn't talked in 14 years. Kathi said she told her sister that, despite the anger she had felt toward her, it didn't matter any more. What was most important was that they find a way to love each other better right now.

I was overwhelmed by what she did. This kind of reward makes up for the missed family events, turbulent plane rides, and the self-doubt I experience as a result of my work as a speaker. When I asked Kathy what triggered her to make the call, she said it was when I talked about my relationship with my mother and the questions I wasn't able to ask her before her passing. "But what made me *run* to the phone," she emphasized, "were two questions you asked, 'Why do we always wait for a crisis to do what we know we need to do?' and 'How can we love each other better right now?' I realized the clock was ticking."

As we continued to talk, I found out that Kathi was a single mother of three grown children, the administrator of the OB/GYN department at Lehigh Valley Hospital in Allentown, Pennsylvania, and the founder of WITS (Women in Transition Survive), a support group for women. Not only was she a breast and ovarian cancer survivor, Kathi had lost five family members to cancer, four within the past five years. Two sisters were still living, she said, but she had very little connection with one and no contact with the other. It was obvious this was an extremely painful situation for Kathi. She said:

> Making the decision to call my sister dropped my anger and propelled me to a whole new level of energy. It was the greatest three-minute conversation of my life. It was like somebody took a concrete bar off my shoulders that I had come to like being there. It sounds horrible, but my anger and hurt kept me going. And then in an instant, all that anger was gone. I know people probably don't believe that and that's okay, but it really can happen. It's not fairy dust.
>
> When I came back my family and coworkers said, "What's happened to you?" They thought I had spent five days at the spa. I never saw the spa. It was a healing.
>
> On our next telephone call, I made a date for a reconciliation day with my sister, and backed it up with a visit. I accepted the olive branch and hoped my sister would. The experience was incredibly healing – to open up my heart to forgive her, for her to hear how hurt I had been over the years, and to gain the courage to ask her to treat me as her best friend. Definitely a quality of life improvement. After all, best friends should

take each other at face value unconditionally and unwaveringly for life. We have moved along. There are still some struggles but we're working through them. It's a period of healing. Stronger. Better. Worthwhile.

Kathi's courage to forgive her sister and herself is a remarkable testimony to the power of letting go of the past, and living in the moment. But there's even more – she allowed herself to be *changed* by that moment. My words may have acted as a catalyst, but Kathi had to take the action to make her life better.

Forgiveness means giving up all hopes for a better past.
– Diane Cirincione

Letting Go Is Necessary for Growth

Today, we'll focus on letting go and living in the moment. First, let's look at letting go. There are so many forms of letting go, with many of them involving letting go of the past. We let go, often reluctantly, of people who have died or left our lives for one reason or another (they move away, change jobs, or embrace a new activity we aren't interested in). We let go (or not) of our youth as we age. We let go (or at least try to) of old loves, bad habits, dreams, guilt, the shame in making a mistake, expectations, attitudes, beliefs, and activities that no longer serve us.

And each time we let go, we experience loss along with its requisite emotions, felt or unfelt. More often these emotions are painful, such as the grief Debby endured with the loss of her daughter, or the disappointment Terri felt losing a promotion at work. But sometimes joy and relief also emerge, as Candace experienced in shedding 50 pounds and Pat felt when she finally left her unsatisfying marriage.

Judith Viorst, author of *Necessary Losses*, a book that was on the *New York Times* bestseller list for over a year, believes letting go is necessary for growth, stating, "It is only through our losses that we become fully developed human beings." Leslie Charles, author of *All Is Not Lost* says the only way to move forward in our lives is through letting go of past hurts and injustices. "It is self-defeating to keep insisting that life is not fair or that bad things shouldn't happen to all of us. Life brings both the good and the bad; and we can move on anyway," she writes. If you are dealing with loss of any kind that is preventing you from letting go and moving on with your life, I strongly encourage you to read Leslie's book. It is filled with compassionate wisdom, encouraging examples, and practical action steps to help you on your healing journey.

> *The hardest part of anything is the beginning, and the second hardest part is letting go when it's the end.*
>
> – Anonymous

If you're stuck in the past, you're likely doing one of three things, according to Alan Cohen, author *Why Your Life Sucks And What You Can Do About It.* Cohen says you're either romanticizing, regretting, or analyzing your past. He says there are only two ways to relate to your past that will do you any good: Appreciate it and learn from it. Like many people, I have wasted more time than I care to write about lost in romanticizing relationships that no longer served me, regretting past actions with my family, or analyzing why things didn't go the way I wanted with a client. My life shifted dramatically when I began to embrace and apply the three laws of appreciation to everything in my life: 1) Recognize the value, significance, or magnitude of whatever you are focused on; 2) Be fully aware or sensitive to it; 3) Be thankful and express gratitude for it. Appreciation allows us to naturally move on to what is better for us because we're always seeking what is of value. As for learning from the past as a way to move forward, I've certainly made my share of mistakes. But since learning about the value of looking for the lesson, when I err, I make every effort it to ask, "What did I learn? How can I do this better next time?" (And if I forget, thank goodness for my compassionate friends who remind me about the lesson.)

Ways to Let Go

- Consciously grieve for a set amount of time every day until you no longer need to. Start with 5 to 15 minutes. Cry, scream, pound a pillow, wallow, rant, breathe, fume, whatever it takes.

- Appreciate the situation. Instead of thinking, "I miss _______ (person, experience, object, vacation, etc.)," say "I appreciate the time I had with ______."
- Write a letter to yourself (or the person) about all the things you've appreciated and learned about the experience or person you want to let go of. If you're not ready to do this, write a "venting" letter first, and keep writing until you get to appreciation. It *will* come if you persist.
- Breathe, breathe, breathe. Breathe the pain into your heart and let your heart soak it away. Breathe yourself into present moment awareness. Follow your breath whenever you don't know what to do. It will always bring you home to your heart.
- Hold a Forgiveness Ritual. I read about a couple that had decided to divorce. They made a list of all the future plans and dreams that wouldn't come to fruition and acknowledged how they would miss these things. They held a ceremony, asked for forgiveness from each other, and burned their list. Then they asked the energy that came from releasing their dreams to help them create new lives independent of each other. You can also do this for any area of your life you want to shift.

Asking forgiveness and forgiving others is a complicated process that involves our deepest empathy, humanity and wisdom. Historically we found without forgiveness, there can be no lasting love, no change, no growth, and no real freedom.

– Dr. Leo Buscaglia

Ways to Live in the Moment

- Complete the past. If you clear up past relationships issues, finish projects, pay off debt, take care of unfinished business, etc., you eliminate the energy drain from the constant reminder that you still have to deal with the situation.

- Practice mindfulness. Stop throughout your day and focus on your five senses. One by one, ask yourself these questions and take a few seconds with each to notice the answers: What do I see right now? What do I hear? What do I smell? What am I touching? What am I tasting? What am I thinking? What am I feeling? What am I doing?
- Realize that the present moment is all you ever really have. You can relive memories and imagine future experiences, but choosing to live consciously in the present moment is where real change happens.
- Teach one of your favorite childhood games that involves movement to young children (one of mine was "Duck, Duck, Goose") and ask them to teach you their favorite game.
- Spend focused time in sensual pleasure – get a massage, eat with your fingers, pet a cat or dog, sing, make love.

Whichever Emotion Is Stronger Wins

When I was a young girl, there was a TV show about the escapades of a dolphin named Flipper. I loved watching that show. Flipper was always helping Sandy and Bud and Ranger Rick get out of trouble and making wonderful noises that sounded like laughter to me. Many years later when swimming with dolphins became popular, I added that to my list of "100 things to do before I die." The day I arrived in San Diego, I headed for the beach and was thrilled to learn that dolphin pods regularly swam where I walked. But a month into my new life at the edge of the Pacific Ocean, I crossed swimming with dolphins off my list. My first "boogie boarding" experience changed everything.

A boogie board is a piece of styrofoam half the size of a surf board that you lie on and, like a surfboard, ride it into shore. I was excited to try this sport because it looked like fun. After a few successful rides close to shore, I went out farther, past the breakwater, waiting for the first big swell to curl. I found a beautiful wave to ride.

On my way back, I wasn't prepared for the huge wave behind me. It picked me up and swallowed me, breaking the safety band that connected my wrist to my board. I tumbled in the wave like I was in a clothes dryer, going round and round so fast I became dizzy. Surfers call it "Maytagging" (as in a Maytag clothes dryer). My head hit the sand bar over and over again as I fought to catch my breath. Panic gripped my body as water filled my nose and mouth. No longer able to tell which way was up or down, my thoughts overwhelmed me, "Oh my God, I can't get out. I'm going to drown." I fought harder, thrashing my arms to get to the surface for air. And then, I had the experience I'd read about: I thought about my family and all the things I'd miss about them. I saw their faces in my mind's eye as everything softened. I thought, "Okay God, I give up. I can't fight this anymore. This wave is too strong." I let my body go limp and prepared to die.

The next thing I remembered was popping up on the surface of the water, coughing, and choking, but alive! I was alive! And telling myself that was the last time I would swim in waves that size, if I even got back in the water at all.

The following week, I received a call from a friend who knew of my interest in wanting to swim with dolphins. "They're back! I swam with them last week. Meet me down at Del Mar Beach at six-thirty tomorrow morning and you'll get to live your dream," he said.

"Um, I don't think so," I said. I had a scary experience last week boogie boarding and those waves are too big for me. I think I'll pass."

"Oh, come on," he teased. "You're going to let one bad experience stop you from swimming with dolphins? All you have to do is dive into the wave on the way out and go with the wave on the way back. It's easy."

"It was really frightening, Ken," I replied. "I'm just not ready to get back in the water yet."

"Okay. Meet me down at the beach anyway," Ken said. "You may change your mind."

"I don't think so, but I'd love to watch."

I arrived the next morning and sure enough, out beyond the breakwater, about the length of a football field, was a pod of dolphins. Ken went charging into the water, urging me to follow. I waved him on as I watched the waves crest, remembering my tumbling experience from the week before. I felt the familiar fear spread throughout my body, until I glanced out at the dolphins and Ken swimming out to them. Oh, how I wanted that experience! My mind flashed to a book I'd read on dolphin communication. The author said that dolphins are telepathic creatures and that she could communicate with them by thought. I figured I had nothing to lose, so I beamed my thoughts out at the pod and said, "If I'm supposed to swim with you today, you come in half way and I'll meet you half way out." I laughed at myself, thinking that I'd truly lost it until the dolphins began swimming in my direction! I held my focus and started toward the edge of the water. As they kept coming in closer, I kept going out farther until I was in the surf and diving under the waves and suddenly beyond the breakwater holding hands with Ken and surrounded by several dolphins.

Ken said, "Tread lightly so they don't misinterpret your movement as hostile. Put one of your arms out in front of you, slip your ears under water, and listen."

As I did, I felt the slippery smooth edge of "Flipper" touch the edge of my fingers and I heard a high-pitched sound of "eeeeee, eeeeeee, eeeeee," under water. For the next ten minutes, three dolphins and two babies swam around us in a circle throwing their noses out of the water and swimming just within arm's reach. It was magical

Magic is remembering the fleeting moment is all.
– Anonymous

And then it was time to swim back to shore. I felt the fear rise up again, but I was so inspired by the dolphins that I just gave myself to the wave and rode it in like I was one of them. I made it back to shore safely, grateful to be alive, and elated to have swam with these spectacular ocean angels. Later, when I reflected on how I broke through my fear, I learned something about emotions: whichever emotion is stronger wins. That day, my enthusiasm for swimming with dolphins was greater than my fear of drowning. Now, whenever I am confronted with something that feels overwhelming or frightening, I ask myself where the enthusiasm is hidden. If I can focus on the enthusiasm and the anticipated prize, I can move through the fear and experience the precious present. So can you. Let go and live in the moment.

To "let go" is not to adjust everything to my desires, but to take each day as it comes, and cherish myself in it. To "let go" is to fear less, and love more.
– Anonymous

Today's Action Step

Write two forgiveness letters – one to yourself and one to someone else you would like to forgive or want to forgive you. Pour your heart out until your soul feels cleansed. Then create a burning ritual for your letters. As much as you may want to send the letters or keep them, *don't.* Burn them and allow yourself to "let go and live on." This can be especially helpful if the other person is resistant to reconnecting or has passed on.

Tips for Creating More Enthusiasm

- ❑ Make a list of all the people you need to forgive. Choose one person you're willing to forgive. When you think of this individual, say to yourself, "I forgive you (say their name) and I release you ('to the Holy Spirit' if you want to invoke your spiritual source). You are free, and I am free, and I am grateful." Whenever you think of this person, repeat this statement and then ask yourself if there is anything you can do to make the situation better. Listen for the answer and be willing to take action.
- ❑ When you find yourself in resistance, notice your body posture. You will often be standing with legs locked, or sitting with arms and legs crossed and face in a scowl. Relax your arms and legs. Smile. While you're thinking of what you're resisting, if you're standing, take two steps forward. If you're sitting, get up. Take a walk. It may seem strange to do this but your movement tells the body that you can move on in your life.
- ❑ Make a list of ten ways that you experience living in the moment (watching the sunset, running, laughing, eating!).
- ❑ Plan a day of spontaneity. Make no plans, just allow yourself to flow with whatever delights you.
- ❑ Buy a camera and take pictures throughout your day of all the simple things you do. Make a small booklet out of them and title the cover page *Living in the Moment by (your name).*

Questions to Ask Yourself

- Who are you glad you forgave and what was the outcome?
- Who is one person whom you'd like to clear up something from the past? What is one step you can take to start that process?
- What is one habit, thought, or trait you'd like either release or embrace? How would your life be different if you released or embraced this part of you?
- What is one of the best things that has happened to you as a result of embracing a fear?
- Who is someone you know who is "present in the moment" and what can you adapt from their attitude and/or behavior to be more present in your life?

Day 20

Nurture Your Support System

How many friends would you feel comfortable calling at 3 a.m. if you needed emotional support?

a. Does my psychiatrist count?

b. I wouldn't feel comfortable calling friends in the middle of the night. I'd just suffer through it.

c. Is this similar to, "How many friends does it take to screw in a light bulb? Five, because if you burn out one, you still have four left."

d. I got smart. I'm in a women's support group that gets together or talks on the phone for an hour once a week, so I'd say seven.

~ ~ ~ ~ ~ ~ ~ ~ ~ ~

When I was a girl and I'd get scared or hurt, my mother would put her hand in mine and say, "When it hurts squeeze my hand and I will tell you that I love you." Her handholding ritual is one of my earliest and most treasured memories of feeling supported during difficult times. Four decades later, having experienced a divorce, career setbacks, cancer (cured), surgery, and deaths of family and friends – I can attest to the importance of maintaining a strong support system. My family and friends have been there for me when I couldn't be there for myself.

Being deeply loved by someone gives you strength; loving someone deeply gives you courage.

– Lao Tzu

I am currently single with no children of my own. I often wonder about what my life will look like 30 years from now when I am 80. Fifteen years ago I jokingly created the idea of a Blue Rinse Nursing Home and Café with friends. It was my way of saying, "I love our friendship and want you in my life forever." At the time I was in my mid 30s and didn't think about growing old alone. But now, as 50 approaches, there are quiet moments in the middle of the night when I can't sleep. I wonder who will be there for me if I am no longer able to take care of myself. I then remind myself to call my five nephews in the morning and enthusiastically tell them their "Auntie Mary" loves them very much.

Our Survival Depends on the Healing Power of Relationships

Nurturing your support system encourages enthusiasm. People feel happier when they feel cared for. But a support system isn't just a "feel good" strategy; it also impacts your health, relationships, career and, in some cases, whether you live or die.

Dr. Dean Ornish, a pioneer in health research and author of *Love and Survival: The Scientific Basis for the Healing Power of Intimacy,* writes:

> Our survival depends on the healing power of love, intimacy, and relationships. As individuals. As communities. As a country. As a culture. Perhaps even as a species. I am not aware of any other factor in medicine – not diet, not smoking, not exercise, not stress, not genetics, not drugs, not surgery – that has a greater impact on our quality of life, incidence of illness, and premature death from all causes.

If our survival is dependent on our relationships, then doesn't it make sense to hold these treasured connections close to our hearts and in the forefront of our choices and activities? How often do you hear of families, workplaces, and even countries that are splintered and broken due to a lack of caring attention and less-than-enthusiastic efforts to respect – and celebrate – healthy relationships?

A healthy relationship implies connection and reciprocity: You and I are in this together and we will help each other. Sometimes I will give more and you will take more and sometimes you will give more and I will be on the receiving end. Striking that delicate balance between giving and receiving is often a challenge in our busy, complex, overworked, time-starved world. We tell ourselves, "It's easier if I just do it myself," or "They don't have time. I don't want to bother them," or "If I ask for help, what will I have to give in return?"

Women, and perhaps even more so, men, have difficulty asking for help. I recently heard that the reason the prophet Moses was in the desert for 40 years was because he couldn't bring himself to ask for directions. (Time for a 16-second smile break.)

Asking for Help is Good Self-Care

Traditionally, women are family caregivers and often forget about their own needs, risking their health as a result. We don't realize that asking for help is a good thing. My colleague and friend Karen Rowinsky, a self-care expert for caregivers and author of *Take Care of Yourself While Caring for a Loved One,* says that asking for help is a key component of healthy self-care.

When I asked Karen to share her personal experience and wisdom about asking for help, she said this:

> I have a very strong community of friends who saved my life. My husband, Max, was ill for six years and died after receiving two liver transplants. We had just moved to a new city when he got sick. I was working full-time, caring for two children and Max. There was no time to make friends in my new surroundings. When Max died I had no idea how to put my life back together. I finally figured out that I had to ask for help beyond my long-time friends or I'd never get anywhere.
>
> It started with the barbeque grill. Max loved to barbeque hamburgers. After he died, I wanted to continue the tradition, but couldn't bring myself to use his Weber grill because it made me so sad. We didn't have Max and we didn't have his hamburgers. So six months after he died, I decided I'd create a new twist on the tradition and buy a gas grill. After going to four stores and walking out because I couldn't get through a sentence without crying, I finally called an acquaintance I had recently

met. She was more than happy to help. She went to the store with me, did all the talking, and helped me set up the grill. The funny thing is that after all that effort, the new grill never made great hamburgers. A year later I went back to using Max's grill. But I had gained a friend in the process.

Following the barbeque grill experience, I stopped trying to do everything myself and began taking more risks to reach out. I joined a support group. I asked two couples to help me make financial decisions. I asked for widow lessons from a wonderful woman I met who had lost her husband at an early age too. She taught me how to date again and introduced me to Match.com, where I met my new husband Rick.

You Give A Gift When You Ask For Help

Karen offers valuable insight into why others need you to ask for their help.

- You give a gift when you ask for help. The people you ask feel important, useful and, in many cases, honored that you approached them.
- People often hesitate to ask for help because they don't want to be a burden. Or they fear being judged as weak, not organized, etc. Yet if you think about when someone has asked you for help, did you find yourself making a judgment about him or her? Most likely your mind starts clicking to what you can do. If you can't help, you even feel guilty that you can't be there. How many times when you discovered that a family member had a hardship or challenge have you said, "Why didn't you ask for help?"
- People can't do everything for themselves. It's actually a bit narcissistic to think you can and not ask for help when you need it. Ask for help.

Healthy people are people who know when to ask for help.
– Myra Mae Van Uxem, Therapist

Who Is Your "Factor of Five?"

Everyone needs a "Factor of Five." Therapists tell us we need a minimum of five good friends in our lives to stay healthy. To help you anchor the importance of these people in *your* life, I'd like you to hold up your hand and look at your fingers. As you count off finger-by-finger starting with your thumb, imagine the faces of five people you would feel comfortable calling at three o'clock in the morning.

Now recount them again on your fingers one by one. Get a picture in your mind again of their faces and imagine one by one you are looking each one of these people in the eyes. See yourself enthusiastically telling all of them that you love them and how important they are to you. Now go do it in person or by phone, one a day for the next five days. Don't worry about embarrassing yourself or them. Even if they resist you, they'll be secretly flattered and you'll have reconnected with your support network. Appreciating each individual will also ensure that if you burn one out from venting your problems, you still have four friends remaining. (Time for a 16-second smile break!)

> *It is not so much our friends' help that helps us as the confident knowledge that they will help us.*
>
> – Epicurus

If you don't have five people in your nurturing network, your goal over the next year is to develop your "Factor of Five." Reach out into your community, visit your neighbors, take a class, join a club or hobby group. And remember to stay in touch with extended family and friends from your past. Using online searches make it easier to locate old friends from elementary and high school.

By the way, it's a good idea to let these five people know they are on your list so if something happened, they would answer the phone in the middle of the night. In return, offer to be a late-night resource for them.

What Is the Best Kind of Support Network?

There are several types of formal support systems that can help you during difficult times. For personal support such as counseling, contact your local hospital or newspaper. Both have excellent lists of resources available. Do an online search for the issue you're dealing with, or look to family members or friends you may not have considered.

Rita Emmett, the procrastination expert you met in Day 3, says that asking for help is one of the biggest things she procrastinates about. When she mentioned to her daughter-in-law that she was feeling overwhelmed with her upcoming travel and holiday schedule, her daughter-in-law suggested that Rita ask her daughter to shop for holiday gifts for the family. Rita said, "I hadn't even considered it. My daughter was thrilled – who doesn't love to shop with her mother's money? She did a terrific job and even came in under budget."

For career issues, join a professional organization or start a mastermind group. You may want to check with your workplace employment counseling services or human resources department. One month after I conducted a Customer and Employee Appreciation program for a client, one of the managers called me and said, "Mary, we didn't believe an 'appreciation meeting' would make that big a difference, but we did what you suggested and it worked. Every Friday we get together and do a half-hour of enthusiastic appreciation at our staff meeting. Our meetings used to center around all the problems. Now people work out problems before coming to the meeting so they can get more appreciation time at the meeting."

As a preventative measure and simply to maintain good health, join an online community such as www.iVillage.com or pay a visit to www.speakingofwomenshealth.com to find a women's health event in your area. Or try another of my personal favorites – join a laughter support group. You can find a "Laughter Club" at www.laughteryoga.org. If there isn't one in your city, start your own laughter club.

Helpers Are Healthier and Live Longer

Whether you've lost a loved one, are simply on overload, or still uncomfortable calling on your support team, remember this: By asking for help, you're actually helping others stay healthier and potentially extending their lives by as much as five years. It's called "Helper's High." Older people who lend a hand to friends, neighbors, or relatives – even if it amounts to little more than helping out around the house – reduce their risk of dying by nearly 60 percent compared to those who never offer help, according to researchers at the University of Michigan. Imagine if instead of just donating money or doing lip service, we enthusiastically embraced and encouraged "Helper's High" at an early age, how much longer we might live and how much healthier we'd be as a global community.

Nurture your support systems. Ask for help. Save a life.

> *You cannot do it all alone. And why try? There is real magic in each person you know, and that magic is multiplied by the people your people know. All that magic is just waiting to be tapped, to enliven your life and help you fulfill your dreams.*
>
> – Jennifer Louden

Today's Action Step

Sometimes the best support group is right in front of your eyes and just needs rejuvenating.

Option 1: Select some of your family members, friends, or coworkers. Ask them how they like to be appreciated. Take notes and then do something that makes them feel appreciated.

Option 2: Ask someone for help. If you normally hire a babysitter, ask a neighbor to watch the children for an hour while you get your nails done. If you're running late on a project, ask a coworker to pick up lunch for you (do pay for it, of course).

Tips for Creating More Enthusiasm

- ❑ Be lavish (but authentic) with your praise. Acknowledge, appreciate, affirm, and encourage them. Ask for help.
- ❑ Arrange to have a fun photo or video taken of your family and support system doing the 30-second laugh.
- ❑ Call your hospital and ask what support programs are available. Visit a few and see what it feels like.
- ❑ Join an online support group. In particular, www.ivillage.com has many message boards that are helpful. Another excellent one is Cheryl Richardson's "Life Makeover" online community. www.cherylrichardson.com/ lifemakeover.html
- ❑ Start a monthly support group of your own. Have a potluck meal once a month and rotate at friends' houses.

Questions to Ask Yourself

- With whom do you share good and bad news, laugh, cry, and feel accepted?
- When you have a problem and need advice, to whom do you go?
- What needs do you have that are not being met? Which of these needs are most important to you now?
- Who could help you meet your needs if you were to risk asking?
- Who have you resisted helping in the past and would be willing to help now?

Day 21

Appreciate and Celebrate Yourself

What do you say when someone compliments you?

a. *Are you kidding?*

b. *Don't thank me. Thank my team.*

c. *Thank you.*

d. *Thank you for noticing. Is there anything else?*

~ ~ ~ ~ ~ ~ ~ ~ ~ ~ ~ ~

There's a wonderful cartoon strip, *Arlo and Janis,* which brings home the importance of appreciating and celebrating yourself. Arlo and Janis are a married couple, at home after a hard day at work. Arlo is reading the paper as Janis says to him, "Arlo, I'm so fat!"

Arlo, still reading the paper, responds, "You're not fat, Janis."

Janis continues, "Arlo, I'm so ugly."

Arlo looks at her and says, "Janis, you're not ugly, you're not dumb...oops. Sorry got ahead of you just a little bit."

We laugh at that cartoon because it's so true. We women often put ourselves down in the hope that someone else will build us up. We too easily forget how amazing and beautiful we are regardless of our size, age, appearance, race, education, financial status, interests, etc. We focus on our weaknesses and what we don't like about ourselves instead of acknowledging our strengths and celebrating our successes. Many of us learn at an early age that who we are and what we look like are not okay. We learn self-deprecating humor to deflect any appearance of delight in ourselves or to cover our embarrassment or shame about our physical appearance. It's time to change "herstory," but first we must be willing to change our own personal history.

Saddle Shoes, Hush Puppies, and Self-Esteem

My history involves growing four inches in height between fifth and sixth grade. My feet also grew from a size 7 to a size 10. At the end of the summer, my father planned the annual "back-to-school" shoe outing at Brower's Shoe Store in Milwaukee. They didn't offer much of a shoe selection in size 10 at that time, but they had a pair of Bass Weejun penny loafers I had seen in *Seventeen Magazine.* I *wanted* these shoes! Imagine my disappointment when my father said I would be going home in black and white saddle shoes, size 10. He didn't believe in slip-on shoes because the heels wore down too quickly and cleats, to stop the wear, were too noisy. I cried, begging for the loafers, saying the saddle shoes made my feet look too big. But it was to no avail. In an effort to comfort me, Dad said, "The kids will never notice your feet because they'll blend into the black and white floor tiles at school." The shoe salesman laughed. I clomped to the car in despair.

My first week at school was a disaster. My schoolmates teased me mercilessly, saying that my feet were *as big* as the floor tiles. Seeing me in tears at the end of each day, my father finally relented the following Saturday and took me back to Brower's. This time, he asked to see the gray hush puppies, size 10. "*Gray hush puppies!*" I cried. "That's even worse! I already look like a boy!" My dad, now unsure how to handle his shrieking 11-year-old prepubescent daughter, said, "Just trust me." One again, I left the shoe store in tears, gazing resentfully at my size 10 military gray "gunboats." As we walked out the door, my architect father who lived in a world of design and construction said, "Look at your feet now, Mary. You don't even notice them because your gray hush puppies blend into the cement."

My dad's efforts to comfort my growing gangliness now seem precious to me, but at the time I was angry and self-conscious. I spent too many years walking with my head down, trying to deflect classmates' taunts about my physical appearance.

When I reached seventh grade, I religiously bought *Teen* and *Seventeen Magazine,* and spent hours pouring over the latest makeup and clothing techniques, dreaming about making myself feel pretty and fitting in.

You will do foolish things, but do them with enthusiasm.
– Colette

What Are You Laughing At?

Twenty years later, I was still buying image magazines, only this time it was for my clients as well as myself. I had started a new image consulting business to help others put their best self forward. But even with my new title and new clothes, still inside me was saddle-shoed "Mary Lou," fighting for self-esteem.

I remember one evening early in my new career, an incident happened after a successful day of speaking. I stopped at Sendik's, the best grocery store on the east side of Milwaukee, not just for fruits and vegetables but for meeting people, too. While standing in the checkout lane, I noticed a handsome man, no wedding ring in sight, in the lane next to me. I smiled at him. He smiled back. I was single at the time and thought, "Hmmm, marriage material." In the checkout lane on the other side of me were two beautiful, exquisitely dressed women. I inventoried what I was wearing and began that dreadful comparison game – navy blazer, pink silk blouse, gray skirt, gray hose, and gray ankle strap pumps, size 12 (my feet had grown another two sizes by this time!).

Lost in thought, I began hearing very loud laughter behind me. I turned around and noticed three young girls about the age of 10 in the candy aisle behind me, laughing and having a good time. I smiled at them and they laughed even harder. Having recently learned that one of the ways to increase self-esteem was to laugh with others, I said to the girls, "Oh, let me in on your wonderful secret. What are you laughing at?"

They immediately stopped laughing. They looked embarrassed. The store got very quiet as everyone waited to see what would happen next. The girls stood mute. I said, "It's okay. You can tell me. When you laugh with everybody else, you have a better time. I'd love to know."

They start giggling uncontrollably. The tallest girl looked at me and then pointed down toward my feet. I felt a shot of apprehension and thought, "No, no, please, not again!" The little girl said, "We've *never* seen shoes *so big*."

Everyone around me smiled. A few tried to muffle their laughter but not enough for my liking! One of the beautiful women leaned over to look at my shoes. As for the handsome man in the next lane, well, let me just say that from the look on his face, our impending marriage was doomed.

On a good day I may have laughed and responded, "I know. Can you believe it? Let's compare shoe sizes." But that night I was tired and cranky. My internal evil twin was thinking, "I hate being embarrassed and I'm sick and tired of people laughing at me all the time. I'm not going to let this little girl upstage me." The next thing I knew, I said in a shrewish voice to the little girl, "You know what? You could grow up to be as tall as me." She threw her shoulders back and said, "I know." I wondered how many times her mother had pushed her shoulders back as my mother did, saying, "Be proud of your height."

My evil twin wasn't satisfied. I spoke again, "You know what else? You could grow up to have feet as big as mine."

She screamed, "Oh, I *hope* not!"

I wish I could have laughed, but I just wanted to hide. I put on a fake smile and walked out of the grocery store. As I drove home, I knew I still had work to do on valuing myself. Just think, I had received a standing ovation that day for my speech on the power of presence, but the memory of my success was diminished by my childhood insecurities. That little girl was telling *her* truth. But that didn't mean it had to be mine. My feet *are* big in comparison to someone who is 20 years younger and wears a size 5. But for me then and today, size 12 was, and still is, just right.

There is applause superior to that of the multitude – one's own.
– Elizabeth Elton Smith

How often do you find yourself reacting to past disappointments, mistakes, and failures that no longer fit the person you are today? Living with enthusiasm is about being able to draw on the part of you that holds your strengths and successes, and comforts your insecurities. Living with enthusiasm is about walking forward with your head held high and a smile on your face and in your heart. Living with enthusiasm is knowing that no matter what kind of situation you're in, you can find the humor and grace to get through it. And sometimes, after enough time has passed and you have found the lessons and humor in your experience, it gives you great stories to entertain others with!

My weight is always perfect for my height – which varies.
– Nicole Hollander

Be Willing to Be Your Natural Weight

One evening, I was watching an interview on public television with Kate Dillon, a "large-size" fashion lingerie model. She spoke of the pain of being an overweight child and how she was made fun of in grade school. As a result, she went on an extreme diet, lost 50 pounds, and became anorexic. Modeling scouts noticed her, but not the anorexia, and she was ushered into the high-fashion world of New York City. She was oblivious to her unhealthy choices until the day she was told, "You need to lose 20 pounds." Already starving herself by not eating for two weeks at a time, she responded, "From where?!" She remembers thinking, "I don't have to do this. Like what have I been doing the last couple of years? What have I been doing my whole life?"

She quit modeling a year later and spent time in self-reflection, sought help for her anorexia, gained 50 pounds, and learned to accept her size. As the fashion world began responding to the clarion call of accepting women of all sizes, Kate was invited back to the fashion modeling world. Only this time she has gone on to great success at her natural weight.

Treat Yourself the Way You Want Others to Treat You

I have a friend who threw a spectacular surprise 50th birthday party for her husband. After it was over, she said, "That was lovely, but I realized I gave him the birthday party I wanted him to give me." Another woman I know kept waiting for her lover to become Prince Charming and buy her flowers. When he wasn't forthcoming, she decided she would treat herself the way she wished he would treat her. She learned that before you can get what you want from others, you have to first be willing to give it to yourself. Since that time, she buys flowers for herself every week. When her lover first saw them, he asked where the flowers came from. In a nonjudgmental tone, she said, "I bought them for myself." Every special occasion since then, she's received flowers from her sweetie and has continued her weekly ritual of buying flowers for herself. She said, "I had no idea how good it could feel to treat myself to something I'd been waiting for a man to give me."

> *I gave up waiting and became the man I wished I had married.*
>
> – Gloria Steinem

Acknowledge and Value Your Strengths

For many decades, psychologists and business management experts believed that a detailed analysis of one's weaknesses coupled with a focused plan to control or eliminate those weaknesses was the best way to encourage professional and personal development. In his newest book, *Authentic Happiness,* Martin Seligman, Ph.D. writes that you should not devote too much effort to correcting your weaknesses. Focusing on weaknesses keeps them in the forefront of your mind (deja vu: energy flows where attention goes). His research shows that deep emotional satisfaction and success comes from building and using your natural strengths. Yet, most of us spend an entire lifetime complaining about and allowing others to demoralize us with our weaknesses. In truth, enthusiasm is more accessible to you when you're focused on your strengths.

Give Yourself Credit

In one of my communication seminars, Carol, a participant and the vice president of marketing for a software company, shared a phrase you'll want to memorize. The VP of information systems brought up an idea for a new product that Carol had excitedly shared with him earlier in the day. Carol was flabbergasted when he never mentioned her name nor gave her credit for her idea. Keeping her cool, she said to him, smiling, in front of the entire group, "Frank, I'm so glad you like my idea that I shared earlier this morning with you." Frank and the rest of the team got the message in a non-threatening way that Carol was the originator of the idea and that she deserved respect.

> *When you cannot get a compliment any other way, pay yourself one.*
> – Mark Twain

Sing the Songs of Your Life

It's not easy to accept and appreciate yourself in a world that has a limited view of beauty and self-expression. People learn these misconceptions at such an early age. If and when you do find self-acceptance and full self-expression – and are singing the songs of your life – the rewards can be enormous. For many of us, sadly, it doesn't come until after many uphill struggles and middle age is upon us. But *whenever* it comes, as Barbara Weiland discovered, hooray!

Barbara is a freelance editor, writer, and pattern designer. She grew up in Colorado in a large family who always sang together during trips to the mountains for family picnics. Although she loved to sing, Barbara was shy and never encouraged to develop her vocal talent. By the time she finished college, raising her voice in song was limited to singing along with the radio while doing the housework. In the meantime, one of her younger sisters went on to become an international opera star.

It wasn't until her early 40s, after a move to Oregon, that singing re-entered Barbara's life. She joined a church where those around her expressed appreciation for her singing voice. When a friend asked Barbara to sing for her wedding, although she felt well prepared for the event, she wasn't prepared for the outcome. "I made a mistake early in the piece, and although I recovered gracefully, my body knew. I felt my legs begin to shake and a sense of panic overtake me," she recalled. She realized that her fear of making mistakes was holding her back. But the positive comments she received from guests encouraged her to keep singing.

Following a move to Seattle, Barbara joined another church and took the next step toward reclaiming her voice. In the choir, she met her now ex-husband who encouraged her to take singing lessons. Her first experience in class was painful. "I got red in the face and could barely sing," she lamented. "The teacher made fun of my discomfort—and I didn't finish the course."

Determined to overcome her fear, Barbara took another risk and started private voice lessons with former opera singers who made it safe to explore her talents without any pressure of "doing it right." At the suggestion of her teachers, she began listening to recordings and discovered her theme song, "I Want to Be a Prima Donna."

When she was later asked to lead a congregational song in church, Barbara noticed she no longer had stage fright. "I realized I had a voice – literally and symbolically," she said. "And ironically, at about the same time I'd made this discovery, I had filed for divorce."

Separation, divorce, and career restructuring became part of her new direction. Several events – leaving her husband and home plus other major life changes that included a hysterectomy – all hit at once. Voice lessons went by the wayside, but not her dream of giving a personal vocal recital before she turned 50. After another cross-country move, a job she grew to hate, and back surgery, Barbara hit bottom. She recalls:

> One night before the surgery, the only thing I could think to do was draw a warm bath and cry. Finally, I called out in desperation, "Please, God, tell me what to do." I heard a voice, loud and clear. "Go home." The decision was made.
>
> I returned to Oregon to live with a supportive friend. While recuperating from surgery and the emotional trauma of so much change, music

came back into my life. I bought a harp and started taking lessons. I returned to my church and joined the choir, then started private lessons with my highly supportive choir director. I started singing "I Want to Be a Prima Donna" in the car and around the house, convincing myself that my old dream was still vital. My 50th birthday had passed, but there was nothing wrong with re-setting my goal to do the recital before I turned 55!

I spent a year planning and preparing for my recital and set the date for a Sunday, just before my 55th birthday. Because I have learned that dreams do come true if you take action, the theme for the recital was "Wishes and Dreams." The repertoire featured 22 pieces of music, including opera, art songs, and Broadway numbers. I rented a chapel that had been converted into an intimate theater and invited 100 family members and friends from around the country.

The night of the recital, the 96-seat theater was nearly filled. The husband of a dear friend made a videotape of the event. The music director from my new church played the piano while guests arrived. My minister introduced me with a prayer and then surprised me by saying, "Let's give Barbara a standing ovation as she walks in." Dressed in the form-fitting white beaded gown I had purchased for my entrance, I felt on top of the world and walked out into the arms of my family of choice. I couldn't fail because I was so supported by people clapping, supporting, and loving me.

One of the most important songs ended the first half – "Birthday" by Christina Rosetti. It was about the birthday of my new life. I knew I had found my authentic voice as I sang the last song – "I Want to Be a Prima Donna." At the end of the recital during an emotional vocal tribute to my audience, I had to stop. My comment, "Oh, let's just start over!" was met with loving laughter and applause!

At the reception, we enjoyed an elegant wedding cake I had ordered to represent the new self I was marrying. I had a smile on my face for the next month. It was such an incredible accomplishment – the first time since college that I had set a major goal and followed through.

This success was due to setting an intention, committing to practice every day, and planning well. The changes in me have been astounding and inspire me to go forward with a new musical goal – yet to be decided! And one of the most fun parts: When friends call now, they say, "Hi, Diva."

Barbara's story is such a great example of turning life's challenges into successes. She is also a marvelous role model for taking action on the ideas we've covered over the past seven days: know what's important, choose your path, renew your spirit, act on your dreams, let go and live in the moment, nurture your support systems, and appreciate and celebrate yourself. As Barbara's example shows, when you practice this **21-Day Smile Diet** with the intent to appreciate and celebrate yourself, even in difficult times, you can recover. You can go on to experience more joy and satisfaction than you thought possible.

You are a gift. Celebrate yourself!

> *And as we let our own light shine, we unconsciously give other people permission to do the same. As we're liberated from our own fear, our presence automatically liberates others.*
>
> – Marianne Williamson

Today's Action Step

List four strengths, characteristics, qualities, talents, and/or skills that you appreciate in yourself. If you have difficulty coming up with four, ask four friends to list four strengths they see in you.

______________________ ______________________

______________________ ______________________

How did you feel as you did this exercise? Satisfied? Uncomfortable? Frustrated? Encouraged? I suggest you transfer your list onto Post-it notes and three 3x5 index cards. Put one card on your car dashboard, the second on your bedside table, and the third on your bathroom mirror (or refrigerator or anywhere you'll see it on a regular basis). Read the list out loud to yourself every day, saying, "I, (your name), acknowledge and value my…" until you have it memorized. You want to be able to feel so confident when you're asked about your strengths that the words flow off the tip of your tongue. If you want to reinforce your strengths even more, ask a friend to read your list to you saying, "(Your name), I appreciate you for..." and then respond after each strength with a "Thank you. Is there anything else?"

Tips for Creating More Enthusiasm

- ❑ Every day for the next 21 days, write in your journal one aspect of yourself you appreciate. Write out a one-sentence affirmation, such as "I love that I'm creative." As you go through your day and find yourself in self-criticism, making a mistake, or simply being irritable, take a three-second time-out. Pause, inhale, make a genuine smile, and state your affirmation to yourself.
- ❑ Write yourself the love letter you always wished you'd received. Buy a beautiful card or piece of stationery and envelope, and mail it to yourself. Or, write yourself an e-mail and send it.
- ❑ Plan something wonderful to do for yourself once a month for the next 12 months and write it in your planner. Your mind loves having things to look forward to.
- ❑ Pamper yourself. Stay at a local hotel or bed and breakfast and/or plan a day or evening of celebrating yourself. Take a long bubble bath with candles, aromatherapy, fix yourself breakfast in bed.
- ❑ Buy yourself flowers and have them sent to you. Ask the florist to sign the card with something special that you've always wanted to hear.

Questions to Ask Yourself

- What do you love most, or are you most proud of, about yourself?
- What positive traits did you inherit from your mother and father?
- What three things can you do to appreciate yourself more?
- What is your favorite outfit? Which piece of clothing makes you feel beautiful? (If you don't have one, it's time to buy one.)
- How do you like to be appreciated? Let people know what you like. It makes it easier to buy you a gift.

Epilogue

This morning on my walk at Torrey Pines Beach, I wondered about you. I wondered what was helpful to you from *Living with Enthusiasm* and I wondered what you will do with this **21-Day Smile Diet**.

At the end of my seminars, I always ask people to identify something they learned and one idea they will act on. I think it's also useful to do this when we finish books. It's a way to appreciate where we've been and a way to shape our future.

For me, I learned again how important a support system is. I remain touched by the generosity of so many who offered stories, ideas, and encouragement. As for the future, I am excited about starting a laughter club and having more online contact with you via my website.

What about you? Take a few minutes to review the pages in this book and your journal and then answer these questions:

- What story most touched you and why?
- What was most helpful to you and why?
- What idea, action step, tip, or question will you take action on?

I invite you to share your answers with me. But most importantly, I encourage you to take daily action to keep enthusiasm alive in your life. These principles work. But you have to use them. So give them a chance, commit to them for 21 days, and see for yourself the difference they make. Know that the more you use them, the more purpose, energy, success, joy, and love you will have in your life.

Live with enthusiasm, count your blessings, and stay in touch.

Valuable Resources

I invite you to visit my web site or contact me at one of the addresses below for the following information:

- Updated list of resources including books, magazines, news articles, Web sites, more inspiration and information
- Support services, research (including permissions) cited
- Information on speaking engagements, teleseminars, coaching, media interviews, articles, and excerpts for your publications
- FREE monthly e-newsletter *Inspired Results*
- Order signed gift copies of *Living with Enthusiasm* and other resources

I'd love to hear from you!

I welcome your stories, comments, questions, answers, and how you used the techniques and questions in this book. Please contact me at:

Web site: http://www.marymarcdante.com
E-mail address: mary@marymarcdante.com
Postal address: P.O. Box 2529, Del Mar, CA 92014
Phone: (888) 600-3421

Mary Marcdante

Books

All Is Not Lost by C. Leslie Charles
Authentic Happiness by Martin Seligman, Ph.D.
Come Alive: 50 Easy Ways to Have More Energy Now by Karen Rowinsky
Do What You Love and The Money Will Follow by Marsha Sinetar
Dream Big! What's the Best That Can Happen? A Spiritual Guide to Unlimited Possibilities by Barbara Sanfilippo
Eight Weeks to Optimum Health: A Proven Program for Taking Full Advantage of Your Body's Natural Healing Power by Dr. Andrew Weil
Enthusiasm Makes the Difference by Dr. Norman Vincent Peale
Even The Stars Look Lonesome by Maya Angelou
Everyday Wellness for Women by Deborah Kern
Flow: The Psychology of Optimal Experience by Mihaly Csikszentmihalyi
Heading to the Hospital: 77 Tips for Getting the Most Out of Your Adventure by Kathy Konzen
I Could Do Anything If I Only Knew What It Was by Barbara Sher
Imagine A Woman in Love with Herself by Patricia Lynn Reilly
Journaling for Joy by Joyce Chapman
Learned Optimism by Martin Seligman, Ph.D.
Living Juicy by SARK (anything by SARK!)
Living Life on a Balance Beam: It Helps If You Don't Look Down! by Paula Statman
Love and Survival: The Scientific Basis for the Healing Power of Intimacy by Dr. Dean Ornish
Mastery: Interviews with 30 Remarkable People by Joan Evelyn Ames
My Mother, My Friend: The Ten Most Important Things to Talk About with Your Mother by Mary Marcdante
Peace is Every Step by Thich Nhat Hanh
Seat of the Soul by Gary Zukav
Seven Habits of Highly Effective People by Stephen F. Covey
Take Care of Yourself While Caring for a Loved One by Karen Rowinsky
Take Time for Your Life: A Personal Coach's Seven-Step Program for Creating the Life You Want by Cheryl Richardson
Thank God, It's Monday: How to Build a Motivating Workplace by Roxanne Emmerich
The Art of Napping by Bill Anthony
The Artist's Way by Julia Cameron
The Body Ecology Diet: Recovering Your Health and Rebuilding Your Immunity by Donna Gates and Linda Schatz
The Land of I Can by Susan Gilbert
The Power of Positive Thinking by Dr. Norman Vincent Peale
The Power of Purpose by Richard Leider
The Procrastinator's Handbook: Mastering the Art of Doing It Now by Rita Emmett
The Seven Principles for Making Marriage Work by John Gottman, Ph.D.
Urban Shaman by Serge Kahili King
What Do You Say When You Talk To Yourself by Dr. Shad Helmstetter
Why is Every One So Cranky? by C. Leslie Charles

Why Your Life Sucks And What You Can Do About It by Alan Cohen
Any books in the *Chicken Soup* series
Any poetry by Mary Oliver (my favorites are *Dream Work,* Atlantic Monthly Press, 1986 and *White Pines*, Harvest Books, 1994)

Health Websites

www.crest.com Oral healthcare information. Take care of that beautiful mouth of yours!
www.heartmath.com Fascinating and useful website on the power of heart intelligence to manage stress
www.laughteryoga.org Highlights the health benefits of laughter and how to start your own laughter club
www.speakingofwomenshealth.com Excellent resource for women's health events around the country
www.worldlaughtertour.com Find a laughter club in your community
www.worldsmileday.com/welcome.html Participate in World Smile Day and hear the Smile Song

Experts Featured in *Living With Enthusiasm*

Act on Your Dreams – Barbara Sanfilippo – *www.romanoandsanfilippo.com*
Curiosity and Wonder – John Kalpus/Dr. Discovery – *www.johnkalpus.com*
Dealing with Loss and Emotions – C. Leslie Charles – *www.lesliecharles.com*
Focusing – Susan Gilbert – *www.susangilbert.com*
Fun and Joy – Mark Therrien – *www.bananose.com*
Healing Energy – Kathy Konzen – *www.thehealingplacewithinn.com*
Nutrition Energy – Zonya Foco – *www.zonya.com*
Mind/Body Health – Deborah Kern – *www.deborahkern.com*
Music To Change Your Life – Jana Stanfield – *www.janastanfield.com*
Nurture Your Support System – Karen Rowinsky – *www.karenrowinsky.com*
Overcoming Procrastination – Rita Emmett – *www.ritaemmett.com*
Spiritual Perception – Beca Lewis – *www.becalewis.com*
Spiritual Retreats – Dianne Gardner – *www.insightsbg.com*
Women's Health Information – Dianne Dunkelman – *www.speakingofwomenshealth.com*

Websites That Inspire and Motivate

www.dailymotivator.com – Start your day with an inspirational personal growth message. Check out the powerful word/photo slide show.
www.beliefnet.com – the most thorough website on spirituality I've found. There's something here for everyone. Inspiration quote a day.
www.marymarcdante.com – Inspiration and information to help you discover your gifts, make healthier choices, and realize your dreams.

Magazines

O Magazine – www.oprah.com
Utne Reader – www.utnereader.com

Movies – Some of My "Enthusiasm" Favorites

Amelie
Babe
Big
Billy Elliot
As Good As It Gets
Life Is Beautiful
Mrs. Doubtfire
When Harry Met Sally

Music

Brave Faith by Jana Stanfield. Anything by Jana. Upbeat, encouraging songs and an inspiring voice for music with meaning.

Deep Breakfast by Ray Lynch. Light-hearted, playful instrumental new age music that's been on my favorite play list for over 15 years.

Enchanted by Robert Gass and On Wings of Song. One of my favorites for relaxation.

Fire Within by Libana. Beautiful! Women's chants from around the world.

Fabulous Swing Collection — Foot tappin' favorites and jumpin' jitterbugs from the fabulous Swing era.

Jimmy Cliff by Jimmy Cliff. Life-affirming reggae – includes "You Can Get It If You Really Want It" and "Wonderful World, Beautiful People."

Kathy Smith's Walkfit Better Body Workout by Kathy Smith. A great walking tape – 30- and 60-minute workouts.

Linus & Lucy: The Music of Vince Garaldi by pianist George Winston. A classic for making you feel better.

Pigatude by When Pigs Fly. Happy, toe-tapping music with musicians that truly love life. More information at *www. whenpigsflymusic.com*

Sun Spirit by Deuter. Upbeat instrumental new age music. I fell in love with Track 3.

Meditation Audios

101 Power Thoughts/101 Ways to Transform Your Life by Louise Hay. Make your day more positive and productive.

Healing Light by Jan Berlin, Ph.D. A meditative healing journey – *www.sacredlens.com*

Launching Your Day by Emmett Miller, Ph.D. An eyes-open, while-you-work- or-play meditation to start the day on a positive, focused note.

Enthusiastic Book Production Services

Book Printing – Central Plains Books – Sharon Tully www.centralplainsbook.com
Copy Editing – Barbara McNichol Editorial – *www.barbaramcnichol.com*
Creative Editing – Leslie Charles – *www. lesliecharles.com*
Proofreading – Laurie Gibson – wordworker1 @earthlink.net
Typesetting and book production – Bob Goodman – info@silvercat.com

About the Author

Mary Marcdante is a communications and stress management expert, professional speaker, and author who helps people appreciate their lives and businesses appreciate their people. Since starting her personal development company twenty years ago, she has spoken to over 250,000 people around the world. Her clients include Procter & Gamble, Hewlett-Packard, Speaking of Women's Health, Northwestern Mutual, Deloitte & Touche, ABWA, Financial Women International, and Nordstrom.

Mary is the author of *My Mother, My Friend* and *Inspiring Words for Inspiring People.* She is also a contributing author to four *Chicken Soup* books and *A Woman's Way to Incredible Success in Business.*

Mary's work has been widely covered in the media, including *ABC World News Now, Fox News, Pure Oxygen, ivillage.com*, and in the *Wall St. Journal, Glamour, Modern Maturity*, and Milwaukee's *Lloyd Street Elementary School News*.

Mary is an industry and community leader and volunteer. She is a past president of the Wisconsin and San Diego chapters of the National Speakers Association. She is a grand prizewinner in *Self* Magazine's "Realize The Dream" contest for her work in helping women realize their potential.

For more information on speaking engagements, media appearances, special discounts for bulk purchases or for personally signed gift copies of *Living with Enthusiasm,* please contact Mary at:

Mary Marcdante
P.O. Box 2529
Del Mar, CA 92014
(888) 600-3421
mary@marymarcdante.com

www.marymarcdante.com